Visions and Voices

RICHARD ADAMS

Visions and Voices

Illustrations by Andrew Thompson

EPWORTH PRESS

British Library Cataloguing in Publication Data

Adams, Richard, *1940–*
  Visions and voices.
  1. Christian life
  I. Title
  248.4

  ISBN 0–7162–0454–1

*First published 1988
by Epworth Press
Room 195, 1 Central Buildings,
Westminster, London SW1*

*Typeset by Input Typesetting Ltd
Printed in Great Britain by
Richard Clay Ltd, Bungay, Suffolk*

Acknowledgments

Some of these pieces were first broadcast as late-night epilogues for Anglia Television. The author is grateful for permission to reproduce them in this book.

Contents

Visions and Voices

It Never Rains . . .

Then God said to Noah and to his sons with him, 'Behold, I establish my covenant with you and your descendants after you, and with every living creature that is with you, the birds, the cattle, and every beast of the earth with you, as many as came out of the ark. I establish my covenant with you, that never again shall all flesh be cut off by the waters of a flood, and never again shall there be a flood to destroy the earth.' And God said, 'This is the sign of the covenant which I make between me and you and every living creature that is with you for all generations: I set my bow in the cloud, and it shall be a sign of the covenant between me and the earth' (Genesis 9.8–13).

It never rains, they say, unless it pours – and always at the most inconvenient times, like the day I was travelling a stretch of road across the fens between Peterborough and Wisbech. I came to Guyhirn where I had to cross the river by a narrow bridge. It's not just narrow. The approach to it is up a slope with a sharp right turn at the top, and it was there, right on the corner, at the height of a tremendous downpour, that the car gave a little cough and died.

So there I was, shoulder to the door-frame, one hand through the open window steering the car, trying to push it across the bridge, with the rain plummetting down like Niagara, trickling behind my ears and down my neck; and as if that wasn't enough, there were enormous lorries – long low-loaders with great lumps of agricultural machinery, and sugar-beet lorries on their way to Kings Lynn – passing so close they almost took off my head with their wing mirrors.

But the water was something else. Great puddles that had been collecting for the last fifty miles in the tarpaulin covers of some of these monsters of the road suddenly washed to one side as they turned the corner, and cascaded all over me, to say nothing of the spray they sent up once they'd gone past. I reached the other end of the bridge, hot and sticky with the effort of pushing, with water in my shirt, in my shoes, and in my pockets. I couldn't have been much wetter if I'd fallen in the river.

But, I tell you – it never rains unless it pours. Across the bridge at last, I left the car by the roadside and sloshed my way to the AA phone box, only to find I'd left my key and membership card in the car. The water had even got to my brain! I trudged back to the car, slumped into the driving seat and just sat there. I could have cried!

For it never rains unless it pours, and you can get to feeling right sorry for yourself when it does – when a day that started out badly gets progressively worse. And some people seem especially prone to calamity.

My breakdown was a minor tragedy. Eventually I got home and dried out; but for some people, life seems to be one disaster after another, and you don't feel like blaming them if they complain, 'Why me? What have *I* done?' They feel as though, for some perverse reason, God has picked on them.

The day the rains came down in the Bible, setting Noah afloat, seems to provoke the question. After all, Noah – the goody-goody – was saved while all the wicked sinners were drowned. If that's how God works, then the floods of disaster that overwhelm some people can only be translated as punishment. But I don't think for one minute that's how it is.

For a start, Noah and his flood belong more to the realms of imagination than hard history – borrowed in fact from ancient Babylonian folk-lore – and turned to his own good purposes by the wise and priestly writer of the book of Genesis.

Evidence of a *real* flood – that a real Noah and a real ark might have sailed upon – is sparse and inconclusive. What you have to imagine are ancient Hebrew tribesmen sitting around a camp-fire listening to the story of a flood which, even if it happened, was so long before their time it was remote and irrelevant, except insofar as the skill of the storyteller drew from it truths about God for their own day.

Skating close to blasphemy, the storyteller gives God human characteristics. It's human instinct, after all, to want to destroy the things that offend and distress you. But what he goes on to make clear is that God was not a bit like the ragbag collection of gods the Babylonians believed in, one of whom they pictured as a god of wrath and vengeance letting fly with his arrows of lightning from the bow that appeared in the clouds at the end of a storm. When Noah's flood was over, the bow – the rainbow – *he* saw spoke of a God of peace and permanence and hope, a God who, pushed to the limits – as well he might be by the stupidity that humankind is prone to – never loses control.

Around their camp-fire, those ancient Hebrews would nod as they understood that they were hardly a preserved race of remarkably upright people descended from Noah. That was just the story. The truth was that they were no better and no worse than most people, but whatever their shortcomings, God had no intention of ceasing to care for them. If disaster occasionally overwhelmed them, it was as much undeserved as were the good things of life; something to wrestle with and strive to understand, part of God's essential mystery, but certainly not a deliberate punishment.

It's odd how we never think to ask what we've done to deserve it when things are going well, and even Christians are sometimes tempted to think that God owes them a favour for trying to be good. It doesn't work like that. Christians are just as likely to experience disaster as anyone else. And for that matter, people who aren't Christians get no less joy from life, necessarily, than Christians do. It may make Christians want to moan that it isn't fair, but I suppose if you try to look at it through God's eyes, there's nothing *more* fair than treating everyone alike.

It never rains, unless – as Jesus pointed out – it rains on good and bad alike. He knew. Heaven is the *gift* of God, not some medal you earn by being a good boy or girl. The marvellous thing about the love of God is that even the least deserving – by human standards – has a chance of being forgiven, loved and wanted by him.

Moving Out

Now the Lord said to Abram, 'Go from your country and your kindred and your father's house to the land that I will show you. And I will make of you a great nation, and I will bless you, and make your name great, so that you will be a blessing. I will bless those who bless you, and him who curses you I will curse; and by you all the families of the earth shall bless themselves' (Genesis 12.1–4).

It's an unsettling, nerve-racking business, moving house. You make a decision and suddenly your whole life dissolves into a world of uncertainty and cardboard boxes. The only sure thing is that as the piles of boxes mount, you'll suddenly need some article you've already packed and not be able to remember which box it's in.

And then your own house, reduced unrecognizably by agents' jargon to a *non.est.det.bung.*, opens its doors to the house-hunters' tourist season. Families and couples invade your privacy, ensuring by less than an hour's notice of their visit that the house is in a permanent, uninhabitable state of hygiene and tidiness.

Coupled with this is your own search for a suitable house in a strange town, in the right location, at the right price, the daunting prospect of making new friends and finding out where the shops are; to say nothing of the slow deliberations with which solicitors do their best to enhance the drama and suspense. It's a wonder anyone ever attempts to move. It's a journey into the unknown.

It's difficult not to think of a wandering nomad's life as an easier option, with homes that fold up and stack on the back of a camel, and supplies of meat, milk and cloth-kits that conveniently follow you around on their own four legs.

Abram was that kind of wanderer, a tribal chief some fifteen hundred to two thousand years before Christ, whose tribe was a motley collection of close and distant relatives numbering several hundreds. Whoever wrote Genesis makes no distinction when he uses the name Abram to let us know whether he's talking about the chief or the tribe as a whole. For the purpose of his story they were one and the same, and they moved house – or to be more accurate, they struck camp, loaded their tents and belongings on their animals and headed west.

Their habit was to wander, it's true, but in fact they rarely ventured beyond the limits of a regular patch. No matter; the voice said 'Go', so obediently, the storyteller says, they went. With no particular destination in mind, they were destined, nonetheless, to be the forefathers of a great nation. From the ancient lands of Sumer on the northern coast of the Persian Gulf, they travelled over fifteen hundred miles to settle in the land we now call Israel. It was the infancy of Jewish history.

But it's all very well for a storyteller, looking back and seeing how things turned out to suggest that it's what God had intended all along. Was he *there* when Abram heard the voice saying 'Go'? How *do* people hear the voice of God?

Certainly people move house for all sorts of reasons; to get away from obnoxious neighbours, to take up a new job, to find more space for a growing family, or to be nearer to ageing parents; but that's not the voice of God, that's simply circumstances – or is it?

You don't actually need to *hear* the voice of God as though you'd just tuned into him on Radio 4. The remarkable thing about Abram is that, living in Sumeria, he would have been open to belief in all sorts of pagan gods, and only the storyteller, with the benefit of hindsight, was free to say that it was God who gave the order. Abram might well have called it gut-reaction or an instinct for adventure.

When the circumstances in your life seem to indicate the need for change, when an idea grabs your imagination, or when the prospect of achievement seems to make a risk worth taking, then God, whichever friend or colleague or situations vacant column speaks on his behalf, is making himself quite plain.

Like Abram, the final destination may be quite unknown. House sales or purchases may fall through, job applications may lead to dead ends; but centuries later, in the letter to the Hebrews, Abram was commended, not for knowing exactly where he was going, but for his faith in daring to set out.

Staircase

Jacob left Beersheba, and went toward Haran. And he came to a certain place and stayed there that night because the sun had set. Taking one of the stones of the place, he put it under his head and lay down in that place to sleep. And he dreamed that there was a ladder set up on the earth, and the top of it reached to heaven; and behold the angels of God were ascending and descending on it! And behold, the Lord stood above it and said, 'I am the Lord, the God of Abraham your father and the God of Isaac; the land on which you lie I will give to you and to your descendants; and your descendants shall be like the dust of the earth, and you shall spread abroad to the west and to the east and to the north and to the south; and by you and your descendants shall all the families of the earth bless themselves. Behold, I am with you and will keep you wherever you go, and will bring you back to this land; for I will not leave you until I have done that of which I have spoken to you.' Then Jacob awoke from his sleep and said, 'Surely the Lord is in this place; and I did not know it.' And he was afraid, and said, 'How awesome is this place! This is none other than the house of God, and this is the gate of heaven' (Genesis 28.10–17).

I played truant once. Now there's an admission to make for someone who eventually grew up to be a teacher! But it *was* just the once. My friend Timmy Beavers and I decided that a double period of Biology with Mr. Liddisbergh was an ordeal we couldn't face. Mr. Liddisbergh was a student teacher with a brain so tightly packed with biological knowledge he was quite unable to prise it out and communicate it in any form that was intelligible or interesting to a class of twelve-year-old boys. So we walked out of the school gate and headed for the sweet shop.

Stocked up with enough long-lasting wine gums to see us through the afternoon, we climbed a fence and scampered furtively across a field to a hole in the back garden fence of the house where I lived. We let ourselves in and wasted the afternoon away chewing solidly through our supply of wine gums, and discovering that the prospect of an afternoon of freedom enhanced by the exhilaration of defying authority and risking parental disapproval was a shabby illusion. Hidden beneath the dining table lest anyone passing by should see us through the window, it was almost as boring as double Biology. The reckoning came next day when the Headmaster sent for me.

'You were absent yesterday afternoon.'
'Yes, Sir.'
'Why was that?'
'I was sick, Sir.'
'You know you're supposed to bring a note if you're sick?'
'Yes, Sir.'
'Bring one tomorrow.'
'Yes, Sir.'

One lie bred another. I persuaded my mother to write the note. It's amazing what a twelve year old boy will do to save his own skin. 'Why didn't you tell me you were sick?' she said. I took a deep breath. 'I didn't think you'd believe me,' I said. I still don't know if she did, but if she harboured any suspicions she didn't voice them. She wrote the note.

The perpetration of such lies and deception and the calculated abuse of my mother's trust should, I suppose, have generated terrible feelings of guilt. They didn't. Instead, I sighed with relief; and talking it over next day with Tim – whose own absence had, curiously, gone unnoticed – I put on a great show of bravado. What did I care if I'd nearly got caught? I got away with it in the end. In my own eyes at least I was something of a hero; and despite the lies and deception of that ancient Bible character Jacob, there's no doubt that in the eyes of Hebrew tribesmen hearing his story as they sat around their camp-fire, he was one of the great heroes of their folk history.

Seeing his chance, Jacob had seized it, cheated his twin brother out of his rightful inheritance, posed as his own brother to deceive an ageing, half-blind father into passing the inheritance on to him; but in the end, con-man though he was – or possibly *because* of it – did a deal with God that secured the future of the Hebrew people.

The bones of it are these. Jacob and his twin brother Esau were chalk and cheese, or to be more accurate, Jacob was quiet and homeloving, Esau was the outdoor type, tough-skinned, sun-tanned and hairy, and fond of hunting. Esau, if only by a matter of seconds was also the firstborn son, a distinction that entitled him to the status and property of their father Isaac when he died.

Sometimes Esau would be away for days, hunting, and come back really hungry. Once he returned to find Jacob making a most delicious-smelling stew and begged him to give him some. 'I'll give you some stew,' Jacob said, 'if you'll give me your birthright.' It was crazy, but Esau was so hungry he agreed.

Jacob's next step – aided by his mother, for he was evidently 'Mummy's boy' – was to coat his arms with goat-skin so as to resemble Esau's hairy huntsman exterior, offer his father a helping of his favourite venison pie – baked by his mother – and so steal a blessing from his father and all that went with it. Once given, this blessing was irretrievable. Tradition said so. When Esau went to claim it for himself, he was too late – and *furious*!

Mummy's boy Jacob took her advice again, and fled for his life, came to Bethel and lay down to sleep, closing his eyes in a landscape of hills and rocks. If you looked quickly, the rocks were like stone steps in the hillside – as near enough a ladder as makes no difference in a dream. Or was it that he half remembered stories he'd heard in his youth – pictures painted in his mind by old men who remembered the Ziggurat temples of Babylonia from which their fathers had come – temples constructed like a child's set of building blocks, several storeys high, each one smaller than the storey beneath? These were images vivid enough to feed the subconscious of a man who, having left the scene of his crime, was still afraid the consequences might catch up with him.

The ladder he saw in his dream linked heaven and earth, and angels were going up and down it. The story-teller, putting words into Jacob's mouth as he awakes, allows him to realize that he can't leave God behind. He'll be with him wherever he goes.

This new vision of an inescapable God is both frightening and heartening. The story-teller's camp-fire audience would begin to understand that the great thing about God is his ability to recognize that in the potential of a Jacob for lies and trickery is an intelligence

which, put to different use, is equally the potential of a great leader or national hero.

It's not that Jacob became a changed man entirely, but that he saw for himself that his ill-gotten inheritance was a responsibility as well as an honour; that what God had made him could be put to good use as well as bad.

The possibility of this is made real by what Christians call the grace of God – a mixture of forgiveness and influence for good that can turn criminals into honest citizens, and more moderate sinners, in spite of their worst natures, into people ready to make a useful contribution to God's world and the people he put in it, so that one day it will become what God wants it to be.

Jacob's vision encourages the Christian hope that heaven on earth is not really as far away as we're tempted to think.

Face to Face

And Jacob was left alone; and a man wrestled with him until the breaking of the day. When the man saw that he did not prevail against Jacob, he touched the hollow of his thigh; and Jacob's thigh was put out of joint as he wrestled with him. Then he said, 'Let me go, for the day is breaking.' But Jacob said, 'I will not let you go unless you bless me.' And he said to him, 'What is your name?' And he said, 'Jacob.' Then he said, 'Your name shall no more be called Jacob, but Israel, for you have striven with God and with men, and have prevailed.' Then Jacob asked him, 'Tell me, I pray, your name.' But he said, 'Why is it that you ask my name?' And there he blessed him. So Jacob called the name of the place Peniel, saying, 'For I have seen God face to face, and yet my life is preserved' (Genesis 32.24–30).

If I'd ever had any notion that appearing on television was the height of fame and glory, my mother soon dispelled it. She'd stayed up well past midnight to watch me performing on a late night epilogue, and when she'd delivered the obligatory 'Yes dear, very nice,' she added the kind of comment I suppose it's only in order for a mother to make. 'Somebody might have told you to put your tie straight.'

But nobody had, and the next time I found myself in the TV studio with a crooked tie, I discovered how difficult it is to straighten it looking at yourself in a TV monitor. After years of looking in a mirror, tying a tie, brushing your teeth, combing your hair, and watching it all reflected in reverse, seeing yourself the *right way round* on TV turns a fairly simple task like tying a tie into a Chinese puzzle. It's easier to close your eyes and do it from memory.

And the camera obviously changes things. Reversed in a mirror you can kid yourself you're quite handsome really. Right way round on a

TV screen tells a less photogenic story. And friends would say, 'You don't look like the *you* we know, when you're on telly.' They were right. I didn't even look like the me *I* knew.

But if seeing *yourself* face to face takes some getting used to, seeing God face to face must be a totally unnerving experience. If it's at all possible. Even the Bible reckons you can't look God in the face and live to tell the tale. Funny that – because there's a story of one man who *did*.

It was Jacob, that same purveyor of sharp practice who conned his twin brother Esau out of his inheritance and fled for his life into the desert. The odd thing is, in spite of his shortcomings, he was no stranger to angels amongst the sand dunes. My guess would be that they were conjured up as much by guilt and fear as any thoughts of glory at the prospect of becoming the founder of a mighty nation; but the miracle is that when Esau finally caught up with him, it was to forgive and embrace him. True enough, he may have taken Jacob's very generous gift of several herds of assorted animals into account; but never mind that, he'd prospered well enough anyway without his inheritance, so it was, 'Hail and farewell Jacob, and good luck to you!'

Jacob must have been more than relieved, but all this was only after a curious wrestling match that lasted all night and gave him a permanent limp. Whether he'd dreamt it or not is anyone's guess, but next morning he was convinced he'd been wrestling with God himself. No – not just with God. This Bible equivalent of the *Mighty Mauler* tells him he's striven with God and with *men*.

Well, haven't we *all*? Not just with every idea about God from *Did he make the word in six days?* to *Does he really care?* but with men and women of all sorts whose hurtful remarks, violent actions, carelessness and greed make us wonder sometimes if there's any love or purpose left in the world, let alone whether God has anything to do with it.

But Jacob, having discovered at the foot of his famous ladder that God was inescapable, was learning now to see him in every kind of unexpected place and person – even in himself. Jacob's *Mighty Mauler* was the embodiment of his own whole life's history of doing the next man down and seeking his own ends regardless – a grim biography that he had to come to terms with and put behind him so as to survive with some self-respect.

Most of us do things we're ashamed of. By accident, or worse, by design, we hurt other people, and even if they're generous enough to

16

forgive us, that's not always enough to relieve the guilt. But there's no use carrying it around like a great sack of self-pity and recrimination that sooner or later destroys every possible friendship and eventually your own soul.

God knows what a mighty opponent of peace of mind guilt can be, and that it has to be wrestled with and defeated; which is why he lets himself be identified with it, and in terrible physical and mental combat thrown out of the ring with it. In the struggle a man comes face to face with the kind of person he is, and with the kind of person, with God's help, he is capable of becoming.

It's a vision of God in oneself that puts much more than a necktie straight. A life, for instance.

Un-beautiful Dreamer

Now Israel loved Joseph more than any other of his children, because he was the son of his old age; and he made him a long robe with sleeves. But when his brothers saw that their father loved him more than all his brothers, they hated him, and could not speak peaceably to him.

Now Joseph had a dream, and when he told it to his brothers they only hated him the more. He said to them, 'Hear this dream which I have dreamed: behold, we were binding sheaves in the field, and lo, my sheaf arose and stood upright; and behold, your sheaves gathered round it, and bowed down to my sheaf.' His brothers said to him, 'Are you indeed to reign over us? Or are you indeed to have dominion over us?' So they hated him yet more for his dreams and for his words (Genesis 37.3–8).

'My Grandad,' Terry Lucas said, 'used to drive the cart that took the lime away.' 'Oh yes,' I said, 'Where was that?' 'I can't remember,' Terry Lucas said.

I wasn't a bit surprised

We'd taken Terry Lucas with about two dozen other children on a school trip which included a visit to an old lime kiln. It was built into a hill up which you might imagine the workers pushing their handcarts filled with marl or clay which they emptied into the top of the pot-bellied furnace. Down below, when the resulting lime was ready, their workmates would rake it out through a row of small arches, coughing and spluttering amongst the dust and fumes in the semi-darkness of a circular, claustrophobic tunnel, the lime they breathed in tearing at their nasal passages and rotting their lungs so that few survived past the age of thirty. The guide described it vividly, and the children went into the kiln in small groups to imagine the horror of it for themselves.

Terry Lucas was clearly impressed and desperately wanted the glory of having an ancestor who had once belonged to this piece of industrial history, however gruesome – or perhaps because it was so. He clamoured, did Terry Lucas, for recognition, whatever form it took. Five minutes later, as a Lightning fighter aircraft ripped the sky apart above our heads, he said, 'I've been up in one of those.'

Well, he might have been; his Dad was in the RAF, but I found it hard to believe him, and none of the children did. They knew. Terry Lucas had *always* done something nobody else had the remotest chance of doing; or whatever he had, it was always so much bigger or more expensive than anyone else's. And if he hadn't actually got one – whatever it was – then his Dad was going to buy him one tomorrow.

Nobody liked him. So desperately did Terry Lucas seek to win admiration, he never got any. But it was no wonder, when his habit was to make himself feel good only by making others feel inferior.

Was this, I wonder, Joseph's trouble? You'd have thought it was enough to have a father bent on spoiling him to death with special favours and fancy coats, without his needing to boost his ego by making his brothers feel small. And knowing how much his brothers hated him already for being 'Daddy's boy', when it came to the dream he'd had – suggesting that one day he'd be somebody really big they'd have to look up to – you'd have thought he'd have had the sense to keep his mouth shut. You couldn't blame his brothers for hating him. Privileged and ambitious, he needed bringing down a peg or two.

It was ironic that when they slung him, for his arrogance, into a disused well, it was the beginning of a chain of events that ended with Joseph perhaps even more famous than he'd dreamed of. Rescued from the well by some travelling merchants, and sold as a slave to an Egyptian army officer of the royal household, his talent for knowing what dreams meant – which he put to good use in the service of the king – led to his rapid promotion.

Twenty years later, when most of the known world was suffering severe drought and famine, but Egypt – thanks to Joseph's foresight and planning ability – had bulging granaries, his brothers came to buy corn and discovered that the king's chief of state was none other than their long-lost Joseph. After taking time to teach his brothers a lesson or two, Joseph finally reveals his identity, there's a touching reunion, and the whole family eventually moves down to Egypt and settles there. It's tempting to add that they all live happily ever after.

I once knew a teacher who told this story regularly to the children. He hadn't much time for religion or churchgoing, but he reckoned it did no harm to relate the tale of a lad who, in spite of being hard done by, ill-treated by his brothers and sold into slavery, nonetheless triumphed over adversity, made a success of life, and was even generous enough at the end to forgive his brothers' hatred and abuse.

Someone else might see it differently. The adolescent, too big for his boots, that Joseph once had been, whose dreams had shown such sneering contempt for his brothers, hardly deserved to do well. But maybe his brothers had done him a good turn, dumping him in the well from which he was lifted into a life which, though it ended in success, was hardly roses all the way. There was scandal, for instance, with the lonely and seductive wife of the king's bodyguard, when his innocence was no defence against the lies of a spurned woman, and he went to gaol.

Once protected and pampered by a doting father, he was now on his own and the world was knocking him about a bit. He was now the victim of other people's contempt, but understanding comes from being put in other people's shoes and realizing how they must feel. The real sign, in due course, that Joseph was undergoing a change of heart was his refusal to take any credit for his unusual ability to translate dreams. It was, he insisted, a gift from God. At last, taught by the ups and downs of life, he was putting God at the centre of things instead of himself.

It's a hard lesson. Most of us take the joys and pleasures of life for granted, resenting its knocks and bruises as though God couldn't possibly be trying to tell us anything when things go less smoothly than we'd like. But honest Christians would say that you have to accept the rough with the smooth as God's way of shaping our characters and keeping us in our place so that we put him properly in his.

Burning Bush

Now Moses was keeping the flock of his father-in-law, Jethro, the priest of Midian; and he led his flock to the west side of the wilderness, and came to Horeb, the mountain of God. And the angel of the Lord appeared to him in a flame of fire out of the midst of a bush; and he looked, and lo, the bush was burning yet it was not consumed. And Moses said, 'I will turn aside and see this great sight why the bush is not burnt.' When the Lord saw that he turned aside to see, God called to him out of the bush, 'Moses, Moses!' And he said, 'Here am I.' Then he said, 'Do not come near; put off your shoes from your feet, for the place on which you are standing is holy ground' (Exodus 3.1–5).

You can't help wondering what gets into people sometimes. They do the craziest things. *The Guiness Book of Records* is chockful of people who've jumped the highest, run the farthest, eaten the most, sailed the Atlantic in the fewest days, or who happen to be the first one-eyed woman in a fair-isle sweater to hop across a lake of ice on a pogo-stick!

I know! I exaggerate wildly, but I'm sure you know what I mean. Depending on your point of view these singular characters are either heroes or lunatics. What madness, I wonder, gets into them?

In all history, I'd reckon that one of the craziest or most heroic could be Moses. His story's been filmed so many times I'm never sure whether to refer to him as a hero from the Old Testament or Hollywood. He'd certainly hold the record for the longest desert journey ever, all forty years of it. What kind of madness was that? Moses' natural instincts and common sense were both against it. He was, after all, in something of a dilemma. Brought up in the royal

21

Egyptian household, treated like a prince, given a royal education, he owed a great debt of gratitude to the princess who'd adopted him, and to her father the Pharaoh.

But he had other loyalties. His roots really lay among the large community of Hebrews who'd settled in Egypt generations earlier, and whose history and reason for being there the new Pharaoh knew nothing about. He only saw them as foreigners who posed a threat if ever Egypt were at war for, being foreigners, wouldn't it be only natural for them to side with the enemy? So Pharaoh took the precaution of conscripting them into labour gangs like prisoners of war, and forced them to work in slave conditions.

When Moses discovered that he was a Hebrew, rescued from the wrath of Pharaoh when only a small child, by the daughter of the Pharaoh, his sympathies immediately lay with the cruelly oppressed slaves who were, after all, his own flesh and blood. But what of the obligations he must have felt towards the royal house of Egypt?

Things came to a head when he saw an Egyptian taskmaster savagely striking down a Hebrew slave. He lost his temper and killed the Egyptian. Then he had to flee for his life and there was no doubt now whose side he was on. He saw his duty as leading his fellow Hebrews out of Egypt into a new place where they could live in peace and freedom.

Now duty is one thing, obedience another. The struggle that went on in Moses' mind is told in the story of the burning bush that didn't burn away – a profound symbol of God's eternal presence. He heard the voice of God, speaking from the bush, telling him to rescue his people.

He found a whole list of excuses. 'Not me,' he said, 'I'm no man for this job. Why should the Hebrews take any notice of me? I'm nobody, and I'm no speaker, never have been. Besides, I'm wanted for murder back there in Egypt.' But by this time, those who'd been after him for the killing of a taskmaster were themselves dead, and there was nothing but Moses' own reluctance to stop him from going to the Pharaoh and demanding the release of the Hebrew people. So he went.

A remarkable series of natural disasters played into Moses' hands. First the waters of the Nile became polluted. The fish died, the water stank and was undrinkable. Then there were plagues of frogs, flies, locusts and one terrible epidemic after another afflicting animals and humans alike. Moses allowed the superstitious Pharaoh to think of these tragedies as the Hebrew God's way of showing his displeasure at the persistent refusal to let his people go. So, at last, Pharaoh gave in, and the crossing of the Red Sea and the long trek through the desert began – though Moses died before he reached the Promised Land – a judgment, some said, for that murder, all those years before. But he rescued his people. He did it against great odds and his natural inclinations, and I doubt if anyone would have blamed him if he'd turned the job down.

Hero or madman – take your pick. But if you can think of Moses as someone who, faced with a difficult choice, and aware of his own limitations, finally put the welfare of his fellow men before his own, then he was an ancient pioneer of the kind of madness that Christians call courage, commitment and faith.

Law and Order

And God spoke all these words, saying, 'I am the
Lord your God, who brought you out of the land
of Egypt, out of the house of bondage.
'You shall have no other gods before me.
'You shall not make for yourself any graven image,
'You shall not take the name of the Lord your God in vain;
'Remember the sabbath day, to keep it holy.
'Honour your father and your mother,
'You shall not kill.
'You shall not commit adultery.
'You shall not steal.
'You shall not bear false witness. . . .
'You shall not covet. . . .'
Now when all the people perceived the thunderings
and the lightnings and the sound of the trumpet
and the mountain smoking, the people were afraid
and trembled; and they stood afar off, and said
to Moses, 'You speak to us, and we will hear; but
let not God speak to us lest we die' (from Exodus 20.1–19).

The Video Shop was open seven days a week dispensing cassette-packed entertainment to suit all tastes and ages; everything from *Dumbo* to *Rambo* and the *Sound of Music* to the *Sweet Sins of Sexy Susan*. It supplied a cheap, ready-made evening out for those who preferred to stay in with a TV snack and a can of beer, and being open all hours God sends made it easy to return one video and hire another. Ah – but, God didn't send all hours, did he? Well not for Video Shops to open in anyway. 'Keep the sabbath holy,' God said, and put it into the mind of man to invent the Sunday Trading laws – with which the Video Shop did not comply. 'Never mind,' the owners said. If they couldn't run a Video *Shop*, there was nothing in the law to stop them running a Video *Club*. So – on Sundays only – the shop became a club by charging a membership fee, and carried on as before. Cost of membership – 2p!

It's a joke really. But never mind Sunday Trading. There's probably no law anywhere so watertight that human ingenuity can't find a way round it, if it doesn't ignore it all together. When did *Thou shalt not kill* prevent a murder by someone sufficiently provoked or tempted? When did *Thou shalt not steal* deter the resolute bank robber? When did *Thou shalt not commit adultery* prevent a man or a woman running off with someone else's spouse? Laws are bent or broken with a regularity that Moses' tablets haven't a hope of remedying. You wonder why he bothered, if all that smoke, thunder and lightning wasn't done just to inspire the special effects department of Cecil B. DeMille!

I know it's easy, with hindsight, to be critical, and it's a bit of a liberty suggesting a timeless hero like Moses might have got it wrong. But, *didn't* he? He knew that this tribe of people, who should have been grateful that he'd rescued them from slavery in Egypt, were anything *but*; and sometimes, when they were hungry, they complained that they'd actually been better off in Egypt where at least the meals were regular. Was it wise of Moses to leave them to their own devices at the foot of Mount Sinai?

Searching for some far-off Promised Land, they'd been trekking through the desert for years, growing tired, impatient, and lacking the security of a settled existence. And with a perversity more typical of adolescents they were desperate to be somewhere else, but too sorry for themselves to be bothered. It was a vicious circle, out of which – as any teacher knows – restlessness and boredom lead to rebellion. And the last thing anyone wants in that mood is a set of *Dos* and *Don'ts*. Didn't Moses know that? Whatever made him disappear up the mountain into the dark mists of a storm cloud to fashion ten concrete commandments? It smacks of the old-fashioned autocratic headmaster, rarely seen outside his study, except to issue daily dictats on school policy; *he who must be obeyed*, he whom the deviousness of children found a hundred and one ways to deceive and disobey, and often with a determined skill that enabled them to get away with it!

Moses should have known. If you read this in the Bible, it takes him eleven chapters to document the ten commandments and all the hundreds of byelaws that go with them. No wonder the people got fed up with waiting and made themselves a golden calf to pass the time and give them an excuse for making merry. There was a rare old party going on by the time Moses came back. Singing and dancing and worse – they hailed the golden calf as the god that had delivered them from Egypt. No wonder Moses was furious. One of the first commandments he'd written had been broken while his back was turned – *You shall have no other gods before me*. In his anger he threw down the tablets of stone and broke them.

Symbolic I'd call that, a picture of the Law they had destroyed. Symbolic too was what happened next. He burnt the golden calf and mixed the ashes with the drinking water to give the people a taste of the bitterness he must have felt. But then, in a fit of anger totally at odds with his hot-off-the-press commandment *Thou shalt not kill*, he ordered the ruthless slaughter of about three thousand of his fellow-travellers. He'd teach them a lesson they'd never forget. They'd be sorry!

It's the short sharp shock treatment, I suppose, designed not just to punish the law-breaker, but to make a potential law-breaker think twice. The argument of deterrence, that's it; put the fear of God into them. What Moses heard, in his ancient day, was the voice of a God less well known than he is today, and to whom he attributed the primitive emotions and reactions of primitive times.

Gathering dust in schools all over the country are Punishment Books which the abolition of corporal punishment has rendered obsolete. The common feature of them all is the regularity with which the same names were entered in them. So much for deterrence. And so much for law. If the voice of the Ten Commandments says anything at all, it tells us that today's people aren't much different from Moses' people. Laws can never be more than the roughest framework for living because they don't actually change the way people are.

I'd guess that's why, centuries later, that other man of God – not to say man of letters – St Paul, took the rather risky line that Christians were beyond the Law. It had no hold on them, he reckoned, because they were answerable, not to man-made laws which only served to highlight how far short of perfection everyone is, but to God. Whatever they did, had to take account of him first and the Law second; and in promoting this rather subversive notion, he was only echoing his hero Jesus of Nazareth who, more than once, was at odds with the Law because the voice of God that spoke to him demanded compassion for the poor, the sick and the dying, and for people's needs to be his first priority.

And if that sounds like a word of encouragement for those who take to the roads on protest marches, or lie on them in civil disobedience, or apply a token hacksaw blade to the wire fence of an air-base harbouring nuclear missiles, it can't be helped. They must do what the voice of God in them convinces them is right, and hang the law!

But how do they *know* they're right?

You may well ask. Even Moses said one thing and did another; had the vision of a people free from retribution and murder, but closed his eyes to it. Doing what you believe is right can be risky. It certainly was for Jesus of Nazareth whose total commitment to life and freedom, peace and justice – all the things the Law is supposed to stand for – ended in crucifixion. All you can say is that those who have the vision, press towards it with their eyes open, take the risks, and accept the consequences gladly.

Smoke Signal

And the Lord went before them by day in a pillar of cloud to lead them along the way, and by night in a pillar of fire to give them light, that they might travel by day and by night; the pillar of cloud by day and the pillar of fire by night did not depart from before the people (Exodus 13.21–22).

You know it's late September when you approach Kings Lynn and hanging in the air is a strange smell as if a giant saucepan of potatoes has boiled dry and the contents are still steadily scorching on the heat. The sugar beet *campaign* – as locals call it – has begun, bringing to life again the processing plant on the east side of the River Ouse. For several miles around its columns of white smoke by day and the glow of orange factory arc-lights by night make it visible as well as smell-able.

Unlike Moses' pillar of smoke, the Kings Lynn versions tend to be horizontal rather than vertical, knocked sideways by the sharp wind that cuts in from the North Sea, bending them at almost perfect right angles to the tall chimney towers from which they emerge.

I've always imagined Moses' smoke signal perfectly upright; I don't know why when there must have been a wind now and again, even in the Sinai desert, to blow it askew. Still, I'd guess it didn't matter as long as the struggling caravan of Israelites could see it and take direction from it.

The story, long part of Jewish folk-history even by the time it was written down, describes their escape from Egypt somewhere around 1200 BC, their forty years wandering in the desert and their eventual settlement in Israel, the destined Promised Land.

And for those who passed the story on, historical facts were less

important than vivid images, so if I say 'pillar of *smoke*' when the Bible says 'pillar of *cloud*' I'm only following the same tradition. Does it matter? Fire and smoke – or cloud! – were woven into or extracted from the story of the past to help those who heard it make sense of the present, picturing a God who was light in the darkness, and by day a mysterious but permanent presence, less far away and invisible than we might think.

Not that it's all symbolism and imagination. Arab traders and Greek armies were known to have piloted their way through the desert with lighted braziers. A desert after all, is no place to lose one's direction. For there's nothing worse than aimlessness. Plenty of people must know it, from the unemployed to those whose regular employment seems to serve no purpose or under-uses their skills. And I can think of able men and women who've made the mistake of retiring with no plans for filling their pensioned leisure with useful occupation. Empty lives, leading nowhere, too often breed self-pity and resentment.

The Israelites were always complaining. When they were fed up with the endless trekking through the desert, oh how much better they reckoned it had been back in Egypt; but then, it's always tempting, when our lives are going through a desert patch, to look back fondly at what we kid ourselves were the *good old days*. Selective memories deceive us. Even the weather was better years ago – wasn't it?

No. Even if you had a guiding pillar of smoke, there'd always be someone moaning that the fire needed making up or the ashes raking out. But moaning's no help. What the past says, if we're honest, is that we've come to where we are through days that have had their ups and downs, their struggles and dull patches, as well as moments of pleasure and joy and achievement, and it's silly to expect the present to be any different. And that's not being gloomy. It's just being realistic. It's saying there's every chance the days ahead will have good times to offset the bad, sunshine as well as rain. We need both. It's only natural. It's often an uncomfortable mixture, but the working together of pain and pleasure into something that is ultimately good beyond our wildest dreams, is the only vision that makes sense of life.

By the time the sugar processing factory shuts down and another season's *campaign* is over, the farmers of East Anglia have already sown their seed for next year's crop. Life goes on.

Christians, more than most, should know that it does, from seeing the truth of it in Jesus. In him they believe God lived our human experience, good and bad; and what they reckon his death and resurrection make plain is that God travels the road of life with us, seeing us not *round* the difficulties, but *through* them. *Survival* is the word, not least because God is travelling companion and final destination all in one.

You daren't give up hope when, nearly thirty-three centuries ago in a vision of fire and smoke, the idea was born that God knows where we're going, even though it's a mystery to us.

Donkey Work

When the ass saw the angel of the Lord, she lay down under Balaam;
and Balaam's anger was kindled, and he struck the ass with his staff.
Then the Lord opened the mouth of the ass, and she said to Balaam,
'What have I done to you, that you have struck me these three times?'
And Balaam said to the ass, 'Because you have made sport of me. I
wish I had a sword in my hand, for then I would kill you.' And the
ass said to Balaam, 'Am I not your ass, upon which you have ridden
all your life long to this day? Was I ever accustomed to do so to you?'
And he said, 'No.'
Then the Lord opened the eyes of Balaam, and he saw the angel
of the Lord standing in the way, with his drawn sword in his hand;
and he bowed his head, and fell on his face (Numbers 22.27–31).

Friendly creatures donkeys, I've always thought. Goodness knows
why they've got a reputation for stubbornness. Admittedly, my
experience of donkeys is limited to the seaside variety, those tolerant
beasts of burden that used to plod their daily groove in the sands of
Skegness or Hunstanton when I was a boy. They seemed co-operative
enough, even to enduring with amazing patience the screams of small
children stuck on their backs by fond parents, when all they wanted
to do was finish their ice-creams. If the donkeys had objected to the
screams and tears, and the melting ice creams dripping into their coats,
and had bucked and kicked, sending child and parents headlong into
the sea, I wouldn't have blamed them. But no. Patience personified
is your average donkey, the uncomplaining animal treadmill of seaside
amusements, yet, oddly enough, labelled stubborn and stupid.

Pinocchio's to blame – Carlo Collodi's famous wooden puppet who
shuns his books and teachers and thinks of nothing but having a good

time and getting rich quick if he can in the company of rogues and tricksters. Remember the fate his stupidity brought him to? He turned into a donkey. The Blue Fairy turned him into a real boy when he finally showed a change of heart, but I still think it was unfair to donkeys.

Christopher Robin's friend Eeyore is another. If his other friend, Pooh, was supposed to be a bear 'of very little brain', then Eeyore the donkey had none at all. Unfair! Unfair!

I'm glad to say the Bible puts the shoe on the other . . . hoof? Anyway, there's a donkey there with more intelligence – not to say *insight* – than his master. And that's saying something, for his master had a great reputation as a prophet and soothsayer trading in blessings and curses. For a suitable fee he would bless or curse the person of your choice, professionally.

So, somewhere around 1200 – 1300 BC when the Hebrews were returning to Israel after their escape from slavery in Egypt, and were making themselves a threat and thorough nuisance to the tribes of people already living there, Balaam was called upon by Balak the king of the Amorites to curse the intruders.

He'd got it all worked out. Balaam would pronounce the curse. The Hebrews would be rendered harmless or even destroyed. Balak would then have nothing to fear, and just to show how grateful he was, he would shower Balaam with riches and honour. The only snag was, Balaam couldn't do it, though the Bible, leaving us to work out why for ourselves, only tells us God wouldn't let him. No matter. Whatever his misgivings, Balaam still sets out to meet Balak. Off he goes with the two princes who'd been sent to hire him, riding, of all things, a talking donkey.

The story becomes a kind of Aesop's fable and describes Balaam's struggle with his conscience as though it were a quarrel with the donkey. Trotting through a narrow alley between two vineyards, the donkey stops, sits down, squashes Balaam against the vineyard wall and refuses to budge. Balaam loses his temper, takes a stick and gives the animal a good clout. 'You pack that in!' the donkey says – or words to that effect, 'What have I ever done to you? If it doesn't beat all! You've ridden me all your life and now you treat me like this!' 'Well, you've made me a laughing stock,' says Balaam, 'Think yourself lucky. If this were a sword instead of a stick I'd run you through.'

It's only then that Balaam sees for himself the reason for the donkey's sudden halt. There's an angel in the way. 'Sorry,' Balaam

says, 'I suppose I oughtn't to be making this trip. I'll turn round and go home.' 'No, that's all right,' the angel says, 'You go on. Just make sure you say the right thing when you get there.'

From then on it's pure farce all the way, with poor frustrated Balak taking Balaam from one likely spot to another from which he might curse the Israelites. 'Here's a good place,' he says, reaching the top of a hill from where they could see the Israelite camp down below. 'Go on,' says Balak, 'You could curse 'em good and proper from here.' 'Could do,' says Balaam, 'Tell you what, I'll bless them instead!' 'I didn't bring you all this way at great expense to *bless* them,' Balak answers, 'Let's see if somewhere else'll do the trick.' So off they trot, but it makes no difference. 'Can't be helped,' says Balaam, 'A man's gotta do what a man's gotta do, when a man's told by God he's gotta do it.'

And that might just be the moral of the story, if only it didn't give me the uncomfortable feeling that it's history dressed up to suit the story-teller and his hearers. I can just see them round their camp-fire, smiling at the notion of a donkey having more sense than his master, but laughing out loud at Balak, king of the Amorites, playing stooge to Balaam's calculated one-upmanship. In this conceited fable, God clearly favours the intruder against the intruded upon. It's not a view that Christians would share.

In much the same way, I remember the comic papers of my boyhood making fun of the Japanese or Germans in picture stories about World War Two. The British were the super-heroes, outwitting enemies so stupid they hardly needed any outwitting. Never mind *unfair to donkeys!* An attitude of mind that presumes other people to be inferior is *unfair to humans!* It crushes the *have-nots* and leaves the *haves* wide open to resentment.

A few lines from a letter St Paul wrote to the Christians in Rome might fit the bill: 'Do not think of yourself more highly than you should,' he said, 'Do not be proud but accept humble duties. Do not think of yourselves as wise.'

Fable or no fable, like Balaam's donkey, the person you think of as stupid may well know something you don't, or with unexpected sensitivity have seen and understood something you were blind to.

Who's a Hero?

*Now the angel of the Lord came and sat under the oak at Ophrah,
which belonged to Joash the Abiezrite, as his son Gideon was beating
out wheat in the wine press to hide it from the Midianites. And the
angel of the Lord appeared to him and said to him, 'The Lord is with
you, you mighty man of valour.' And Gideon said to him, 'Pray, sir,
if the Lord is with us, why then has all this befallen us? And where
are all his wonderful deeds which our fathers recounted to us saying,
"Did not the Lord bring us up from Egypt?" But now the Lord has
cast us off and given us into the hand of the Midian.' And the Lord
turned to him and said, 'Go in this might of yours and deliver Israel
from the hand of Midian. Do I not send you?' And he said to him,
'Pray Lord, how can I deliver Israel? Behold, my clan is the weakest
in Manasseh and I am the least in my family.' And the Lord said to
him, 'But I will be with you and you shall smite the Midianites as one
man' (Judges 6.11–16).*

If it's late-night horror you're after, you could do worse than go to bed
with the Book of Judges. There's enough gruesome goings-on in it to
make your toes curl – everything from bribery and corruption to
human sacrifice – bloodbaths you could swim in!

It's the book where you find that famous story about the strong man
Samson and his hairdresser girlfriend Delilah. It's a book of ancient
Jewish heroes really, but they all seem to have this terrifying streak
of violence – like the woman who sneaked up on an army general and
hammered a tent peg through his brain! It's such blood-curdling stuff,
you wonder what on earth it's doing in a book we sometimes refer to

as the *Holy* Bible. It's only fair to say though, that not all the heroes actually set out to find fame and glory amidst battle and bloodshed. Gideon for instance. The Book of Judges describes him as a mighty man of valour. In fact he was a nobody from nowhere.

The background to the story is the struggle of the people of Israel to settle in the Promised Land after their escape from slavery in Egypt. They met pockets of resistance everywhere, and hordes of bandits whose daily routine was robbery with violence. Gideon was the youngest of a family of no importance. They belonged to the most insignificant tribe in all Israel; but folk-lore tells how an angel spoke to him and told him to save his people from the regular attacks of a horde of bandits from the Arabian Desert – the Midianites. 'Go on,' the angel said, 'The Lord is with you.' 'Tell me another,' says Gideon, 'If he's on our side, how come the Midianites don't leave us alone?'

This is, of course, something like twelve hundred years before Christ. You have to excuse the primitive notion that God took a special delight in seeing his favourite team knock the living daylights out of their opponents. In any case, Gideon didn't want to do it. 'How can I save Israel?' he said, 'I'm no one special.' But God insisted, so Gideon, trying hard to summon up faith and courage, asks for proof. He wants to be sure he's the man for the job, and that it really is God who wants him to do it.

It takes three unusual happenings to convince him. First a batch of cakes and a dish of broth mysteriously catch fire. Then a sheep's fleece left out all night is strangely wet next morning when the grass all around it is dry. Next day the opposite happens – the fleece is dry, the grass is wet.

Deciding that he can't argue with the impossible, Gideon hand picks three hundred men, and with this select guerilla force he destroys the Midianites. If you want the gory details you can read them for yourself in the Book of Judges, chapters 6 to 8.

You can, if you like, set the moral questions on one side, and find it quite heartening that a nobody, by the inspiration of God can become a somebody – a local, and in time, a national hero of great courage and daring. But what I haven't told you is that Gideon had some brothers – and the Midianites had killed them all.

Now you will see how the call to free his people from the constant threat of Midianite attacks may well have been given its cutting edge by the desire to avenge his brothers. It's hard then to detach his heroism from his ulterior motives. But that's the kind of thought that only comes with hindsight, when you read the Old Testament in the light of the New, where you find Jesus of Nazareth saying, 'Love your enemies and do good to them that hate you.'

Promises, Promises

Then the Spirit of the Lord came upon Jephthah, and he passed through Gilead and Manasseh, and passed on to Mizpah of Gilead, and from Mizpah of Gilead he passed on to the Ammonites. And Jephthah made a vow to the Lord and said, 'If thou wilt give the Ammonites into my hand, then whoever comes forth from the doors of my house to meet me, when I return victorious from the Ammonites, shall be the Lord's, and I will offer him up for a burnt offering.' So Jephthah crossed over to the Ammonites to fight against them; and the Lord gave them into his hand (Judges 11.29–32).

Have you ever had one of those days? You get out of bed and it's raining. You twist your ankle going downstairs, find the clock's stopped so it's later than you thought, burn the toast – and the rest of the day you just stumble from one calamity to the next – one of those days that started off on the wrong foot and you couldn't put another foot right for the rest of it. The sadder thing is the way some people's whole lives seem to be like that. They get off to a poor start and the burden of it seems to dog them until the day they die.

Poor old Jephthah was a bit like that. He's another sort-of-hero from that little book of horrors, the Bible's Book of Judges. Holy book it may be, but it pulls no punches. 'Now Jephthah the Gileadite,' it says, 'was a mighty warrior, but he was the son of a harlot.' The upshot of that was that his brothers and the elders of the tribe threw him out. Having nothing else to do he fell in with a bunch of layabouts whose chief pastime was robbery with violence. Jephthah got himself quite a reputation for it. In fact, some years later, when his fellow-tribesmen needed a tough-guy to lead an army against their enemies, they sent word. 'Me?' said Jephthah, 'You turned me out of house and home. Why should I?' But they pleaded with him, and promised he could be chief, so at last he agreed.

The enemies were the Ammonites, near-neighbours in the highlands east of Jordan. They justified their regular attacks on the people of Israel by claiming that, in returning from slavery in Egypt the Israelites had settled in land that belonged to them, the Ammonites. They wanted it back. Jephthah argued the Israelite case, but the Ammonites wouldn't listen and the argument erupted into violence. Jephthah declared war.

He also took out a kind of insurance policy against the result. Remember this is 1200 years before Christ. The people of those days were quite at home with a God who took sides, and if you bribed him well enough he'd see that your side won. It was a time of primitive religious rituals too, including human sacrifice. What Jephthah put down as a premium for guaranteed victory was the life, as a burnt offering, of whoever was first to meet him when he returned home from the battle.

I can't *think* what possessed him. By this time in the tale he had an only daughter. Yes! You've guessed it. When the Ammonites were defeated and Jephthah came rejoicing home, his daughter rejoiced too, and with timbrels and dances, came first to greet him. Good old Dad! But promises, we tell our children, are meant to be kept, and Jephthah kept his, though if he'd backed down I can't think anyone would have blamed him, least of all God.

Old Testament prophets who arrived on the scene six centuries or so after Jephthah were beginning to glimpse the vision of God that was eventually seen in Jesus of Nazareth. They heard the voice of a loving God saying, 'Mercy I desire, not sacrifice.'

The agony of living is often emotional; a question sometimes of making a choice between honouring a commitment that turns out impossible to keep without causing pain or grief, or instead, pulling out and risking loss of face. It's largely a matter of pride – a question of whether your own esteem counts for more than your love for others.

Who Calls?

Now the boy Samuel was ministering to the Lord under Eli. And the word of the Lord was rare in those days; there was no frequent vision. At that time Eli, whose eyesight had begun to grow dim, so that he could not see, was lying down in his own place; the lamp of God had not yet gone out, and Samuel was lying down within the temple of the Lord, where the ark of God was. Then the Lord called, 'Samuel! Samuel!' and he said, 'Here I am!' and ran to Eli and said, 'Here I am, for you called me.' But he said, 'I did not call; lie down again.' So he went and lay down. And the Lord called again, 'Samuel!' And Samuel arose and went to Eli, and said, 'Here I am, for you called me.' But he said, 'I did not call, my son; lie down again.' Now Samuel did not yet know the Lord, and the word of the Lord had not yet been revealed to him. And the Lord called Samuel again the third time. And he arose and went to Eli, and said, 'Here I am, for you called me.' Then Eli perceived that the Lord was calling the boy. Therefore Eli said to Samuel, 'Go, lie down; and if he calls you, you shall say, "Speak, Lord, for thy servant hears"' (I Samuel 3.1–9).

Ten years old they were, a boy and a girl, swapping stories and child ambitions.

'What do you want to be when you grow up?' the girl said.

'Teacher,' said the boy.

'So do I,' said the girl.

Only heaven knows what happened to the girl, but eleven years later the boy became a teacher. I know that because it was me.

Now teaching is one of those jobs, like the priesthood or nursing, that used to be thought of as a calling. A vocation. Some, with perhaps a greater sense of dedication than others still think it is. What I want

to know is: was it God who called me to be a teacher when I was only ten? I'd thought it was *my* idea.

There's a boy about the same age in the Bible. He became a priest, so I suppose you could say that God called him. Samuel his name was, but when you read the story, you find he didn't really have a lot of choice. A couple of years after he was born, his mother took him to church for a thanksgiving service, and *left him there!* To be accurate I ought to call the premises a *temple*, not a *church*. But anyway, she left him to be brought up by Eli, the ancient priest-in-charge – a pretty rum thing to do really, seeing that the old man had raised two sons of his own whose ideas of devotion to the task of helping him in his priestly duties consisted mostly of scoffing the juiciest chunks of meat from the sacrificial offerings, and playing fast and loose with a variety of girls whose sexual favours were available as part of the pagan fertility rites that somehow, now and again, got mixed up with the more respectable religious ceremonies.

Now all this was ripe scandal and common gossip, and a rare hothouse to raise the young Samuel in. He was no more than twelve when it struck him that somebody ought to tell old Eli what a pair of layabouts his sons were, and how the chances were they'd come to a sticky end.

The Bible story says that Samuel was sleeping in the temple when he heard someone calling him. Thinking it was Eli, he went to see what he wanted. Nothing. Eli hadn't called him at all. Three times this happened. The way I see it, each time Samuel got as far as Eli's bedside, only to find his courage deserting him. How does a young lad, still wet behind the ears, tell his guardian and teacher, who's growing old and blind, that his sons are a couple of corrupt and loose-living good-for-nothings, giving religion a bad name – and has he, their father, ever lifted a finger to stop them? . . . No!

I wouldn't have been in Samuel's shoes for anything. If he escaped with a thick ear and an order to mind his own business, he might have got off lightly. As it happened, Eli himself sensed something in the air. Truth. Truth he'd rather not face about his sons and his failure. God's truth, teetering on the lips of this young trainee priest. 'Go,' said Eli to Samuel, 'lie down, and if he calls you again you shall say, "Speak, Lord, for thy servant hears." ' You wonder which one of them was putting off the moment of truth; Samuel, too timid to tell; or Eli, reluctant to hear.

Moments of truth are risky, like the moment after you've wired in some new electric fittings and you switch the current back on for the first time. Will their be a burst of light or music, or a flash and a bang and a smell of melting plastic? Facing up to what you know you must do, or the repercussions of something you've done or left undone, needs courage.

A Christian would say it needs faith too, for a Christian senses that moments of truth are those when God gives us a glimpse of ourselves as we really are; young, green and hesitant like Samuel, yet full of innocent promise and unconscious wisdom; or like Eli, old and frail and so aware of how easy it is to lose your grip on the things that really matter. I don't think it's reading too much between the lines if I blame too great a sense of vocation and devotion to duty for the separation of Eli from his family and the chance to influence his sons for the better.

Who knows? Even Samuel grew old and made some less than perfect judgments before he died. Well, we're *all* human, but the Christian's faith in God nourishes the possibility that he can make of us something more than we can manage on our own. The original potential which we misuse and bruise and batter, his love and forgiveness can heal and restore so that, at last, it resembles the vision of us that he had at the beginning.

Medium Rare

Now Samuel had died, and all Israel had mourned for him and buried him in Ramah, his own city. And Saul had put the mediums and the wizards out of the land. The Philistines assembled, and came and encamped at Shunem; and Saul gathered all Israel, and they encamped at Gilboa. When Saul saw the army of the Philistines, he was afraid, and his heart trembled greatly. And when Saul inquired of the Lord, the Lord did not answer him, either by dreams, or by Urim, or by prophets. Then Saul said to his servants, 'Seek out for me a woman who is a medium, that I may go to her and inquire of her.' And his servants said to him, 'Behold, there is a medium at Endor' (I Samuel 28.3–7).

'Is there anybody there?'
'Knock once for yes. Knock twice for no.'

The scene is the darkened consulting room of a spiritualist medium. A seance is in session. The heavy curtains are drawn, the yellow flame of a lamp hums gently, the atmosphere is taut with expectation . . . and the medium has gadgets up her sleeve to levitate the table when the moment is propitious. The voice of a departed one speaks.

'Hello Phyllis. This is Desmond.'

Again he speaks, with the slow, echoing drawl of a child playing ghosts in an empty rain barrel.

'Hello Phyllis. This is Desmond.'

Does anyone really believe in it? *Is there anybody there?* If there really was somebody there, they'd have more sense than to knock once for yes or twice for no, and to speak like a run-down clockwork Frankenstein's mummy. Can you really get through to people long dead and gone and hold a lucid conversation? I really don't know, but I doubt it.

The trouble is, when you read of it happening in the Bible of all places, it's tempting to think there might be something in it. Even so, you need to watch out. On the one occasion it did happen, the outcome was disastrous.

The first king of Israel it was, a rather disturbed character called Saul who from the first day of his appointment started to go downhill, rapidly gathering speed as he descended through a history of madness, vendetta, and an almost endless series of wars that finally found him so shot through with arrows that he ended it all by falling on his own sword.

A sad case all together. So pigheaded he rarely took anyone's advice, with the result that on the one day he needed some, nobody felt inclined to give him any. Mind you, he was so hard-pressed there was probably no advice to give that would have been of any use. An army of Philistines, the same mob Goliath had belonged to – you remember Goliath, the *Giant Haystacks of* the Bible, famous for being knocked out with a stone from David's catapult? That one. Anyway, the Philistines had assembled their forces, a frightening array of warriors, bowmen and chariots that left Saul greatly outnumbered. What he needed was a cunning strategy. 'Anyone got a cunning strategy?' he asked.

He tried the priest who did the ancient Jewish equivalent of tossing a coin. 'Urim or Thummim?' he said. Heads or tails? Either way it only told him yes or no, not what to do. So he consulted prophets. No help there. He slept and dreamed about Philistines but woke up unenlightened. All these were recognized ways of finding out what God's advice was in a time of crisis, but Saul had spent the greater part of his career doing anything but what God wanted. It was no surprise to anyone that when Saul called on God, he wasn't at home.

Saul was desperate. Samuel would have known what to do, that wise old man who'd anointed him king. If only he could get in touch with Samuel. But he couldn't. Samuel was dead. So Saul embarked on a last resort. Mediums were against the rules. As king he'd had them banned and exiled; but if he could find one, there was a chance he might get through to Samuel and hear from him some marvellous plan of campaign. So that's what he did, setting out in disguise to

48

consult a medium in a gloomy cavern where she conjured up an apparition of an old man wrapped in a robe.

It's an odd sort of story. I can't help thinking that history's been doctored a bit, just to add weight to the Bible's general disapproval of tampering with the spirit world. *Trust God* is the message, not dubious experiment and superstition. But *was* the apparition Samuel? Saul clearly thought so. It made him quite weak at the knees, though whether that was fright or hunger or both is anyone's guess, but the medium felt obliged to send him away with a good meal inside him. Was it really Samuel Saul had seen or a figment of his famished body and fevered imagination?

Perhaps you know from experience how the spectre of someone you've let down badly can haunt the memory for years. Desperate people, often see only what they want to see, and hope to hear only what they want to hear. Saul was to be disappointed. 'The way you've been carrying on,' the apparition said, 'you deserve to come to a bad end.' And he did. It was only what he must have known already in his heart of hearts.

You can't escape the consequences of living entirely for yourself, thinking that others are subject to your whims and fancies. For a king like Saul, or anyone else in authority, it must be an occupational hazard, though ordinary folks can suffer from it too. We all like to get our own way if we can. Saul's story is an illustration of the private hell, the lonely, burning agony a man or woman can come to when they expect the whole world to revolve around them and leave God out of the reckoning.

Jesus is said to have painted a picture of hell as a place of everlasting fire, wailing and gnashing of teeth. Some Christians find it hard to take. Would a God of love inflict such torment? No, of course not; but that doesn't stop reckless people inflicting it upon themselves. Finally, and often too late, they find they've excluded themselves from the reckonings of God, and a Christian can't help thinking that the pain of such a separation must be hell indeed.

Fire and Water

And behold, the Lord passed by, and a great and strong wind rent the mountains, and broke in pieces the rocks before the Lord, but the Lord was not in the wind; and after the wind an earthquake, but the Lord was not in the earthquake; and after the earthquake a fire, but the Lord was not in the fire; and after the fire a still small voice (I Kings 19.11b–12).

A still small voice wouldn't have been much good in the shoe factory where my Dad used to work. You'd have had to shout to make yourself heard above the din. Presses thumped, heaved and hissed, stamping out leather soles. Another marvellous machine swallowed nails and shot them out again with the rapidity and clatter of a machine gun, and wooden racks loaded with half-made shoes rumbled from one part of the process to another over the uneven floorboards on rickety wheels.

Noise, bustle, industry – a place where my Dad reckoned *real work* was done – the sort where the pace never slackens and your energy drains away by the hour, real and urgent and proving itself by making a heck of a din so's you'd never doubt the sense of purpose and achievement. Something was really getting done. Well . . . maybe.

That great old Bible character Elijah once had to learn that life still made sense and was worth living, even when nothing much seemed to be going on. He was a prophet. That's not to say he was a fortune-teller, but a man with a deep sense of God, an eye for the truth, and the courage to tell it loud and clear when necessary; which is why he fell foul of the queen of his day, the notorious Jezebel. She's the conniving woman who arranged the murder of a local vineyard owner so that the king, her husband Ahab, could use it as a vegetable patch.

Ahab and Jezebel were the plague of Elijah's life. They brought idolatry and heathen religious practices into Israel, enough and more to fill Elijah's life with moments of high drama. It all took place round about 870 BC and was handed down to posterity by way of the Books of Kings.

Elijah waged constant war with primitive rites and the prophets of the pagan god Baal in particular. On one occasion Elijah confronted four hundred and fifty of his prophets and challenged them to a kind of firelighting contest. Each would have a bull slaughtered for sacrifice and call upon their God to light the sacrificial bonfire.

The prophets of Baal worked themselves into a frenzy, slashing themselves with knives in a manic ritual of persuasion with which their god refused to co-operate. Elijah poked fun at their efforts and turned to his own sacrifice which for good measure he had liberally soaked with water. All it needed was a few words of prayer. Fire fell from heaven, and the whole lot went up like a torch.

Legend, fact, or a little bit of both, it was pretty impressive, and confirmed Elijah's notion that this was how God did things – all noise and show. But, not surprisingly, things fell a bit flat after that, and worse, the furious Jezebel put a price on Elijah's head and he fled to the hills for safety. It was there he began to feel sorry for himself. Coupled with a resounding anticlimax was the thought that he was the only bloke left in the world who cared anything for God and honesty and decency. Brooding in the shelter of a cave he waited desperately for a word of encouragement from God – a sign of some sort.

And behold, the Lord passed by, and a great and strong wind rent the mountains, and broke in pieces the rocks before the Lord, but the Lord was not in the wind.

Nor was he in the earthquake that followed. Nor in the fire. For once vivid images said nothing to him. As though he were my old Dad equating factory noise with getting something done, Elijah looked for a sign from God in the noise and drama of the storm and it didn't come.

It was afterwards, in the stillness, when the wind and tremors had subsided, he was able to look at things coolly and calmly. For all that Ahab the king had decreed that the nation should worship his imported heathen idols, a great many people *had* stayed faithful to God. Elijah realized he wasn't alone, nor the only one who cared about truth and morality.

The message in the stillness gave him the encouragement he needed to go back to the city and carry on the fight against the evil and corruption of the royal house of Ahab and Jezebel. Up in the mountains he'd learned how easy it is in the noise and confusion of living, to get things all out of proportion. The still small voice of God, barely a whisper, had enabled him to see things in their proper perspective, and take heart.

Holy Smoke

In the year that King Uzziah died, I saw the Lord sitting upon a throne, high and lifted up; and his train filled the temple. Above him stood the seraphim; each had six wings: with two he covered his face, and with two he covered his feet, and with two he flew.
And one called to another and said:
    'Holy, holy, holy is the Lord of hosts
    the whole earth is full of his glory.'
And the foundations of the thresholds shook at the voice of him who called, and the house was filled with smoke (Isaiah 6.1–4).

Some mornings, the little village school where I used to work was filled with smoke – when the wind was in the wrong direction. It was a case of opening the windows and freezing, or shutting them and choking to death. In the end we let the fire out and wheeled in portable gas-heaters instead.

The place is closed now. I helped to load the desks and equipment into the lorry, and then stood for a while in the quiet empty building. There were hints in the air of polish and disinfectant, dust and chalk and smoke, distinctly and uniquely school smells. And there were pictures in my mind's eye – little groups of children sitting at their desks, a huddle of mothers sitting on infant chairs watching the nativity play, and the child who brought sandwiches for lunch that were such giant doorsteps she was still solemnly munching them when all the others had gone out to play.

It could be that some buildings have an atmosphere that readily links the present with the past. For me after only six years, that empty building was full of memories and images. You could put it down to nostalgia. I'd prefer to say it's a way of looking at things that comes

from having a religious outlook – a readiness to sense in something as ordinary as the bare walls of an empty classroom, an echo of something that belongs to eternity and that enhances each memory, making it vivid and treasurable.

I'd guess that's how Isaiah saw things. The Bible prophet of 700 years or so before Christ must have been into the temple at Jerusalem often enough, yet just this once he saw it differently – its gold and silver ornaments, the fine carvings and rich draperies and – whether in reality or only in his imagination, who can tell? – he saw the representations of God's messengers, and how could they have come post-haste from heaven unless they had wings?

Call them seraphim, angels, or what you will, they were real to Isaiah. Imagination made them so. That's what imagination's for. It can turn the experience of an artist into light and colour on a canvas, or the feelings of a composer into a haunting melody; or in the case of a visionary and poet like Isaiah, it can conjure up vivid images with words. Imagination! Finely tuned, it can turn the commonplace into something special, the man in the street, whoever he is, into a person of worth.

That's why Isaiah was suddenly ill at ease. He knew that Assyrian forces threatened Jerusalem, and saw the prospect of the temple – symbol for centuries of Israel's relationship with God – lying in ruins. He suspected it would be no less than served the nation right for a history of corruption and injustice, but there in the temple, that monument to the faith and devotion of the past, a terrible mixture of history and foreboding heightened his awareness of his own shortcomings.

Woe is me. For I am lost; for I am a man of unclean lips, and I dwell in the midst of a people of unclean lips (Isaiah 6.5).

Imagination can lift you up or knock you down. In the right surroundings it can fill you at once with a sense of awe and a sense of inadequacy from which springs the worship of God.

Imagination is a gift of God which makes a difference to the way you see things. What God has created and cares for is never ordinary. Common earth is holy ground. Imagination re-defines the world we live in – the city streets, the village store, the factory floor are holy places. And the people you meet, friends, neighbours, workmates are holy people, transformed by a particular leap of imagination that I can only call faith. It's the extra ingredient that takes those feelings of awe and inadequacy and adds *responsibility*, for what you think of as holy you must treat with respect – everything and everybody. It's a way of seeing things that would do away with violence and vandalism and any other deliberate hurt, for it knows the value God places on everything and everyone, and understands that all these things are trusted to our safe keeping.

Who, *me*?

Now the word of the Lord came to me saying, 'Before I formed you in the womb I knew you, and before you were born I consecrated you; I appointed you a prophet to the nations.' Then I said, 'Ah, Lord God! Behold, I do not know how to speak, for I am only a youth.' But the Lord said to me, 'Do not say, "I am only a youth"; for to all to whom I send you you shall go, and whatever I command you you shall speak. Be not afraid of them, for I am with you to deliver you, says the Lord' (Jeremiah 1.4–8).

I was young once. I had all the things you're supposed to have when you're young – vitality, enthusiasm, open-mindedness, fresh opinions, new ideas . . . just so that the next grown-up you run into can squash them flat! If you did something silly, they'd tell you to grow up; and the minute you thought you'd done something grown up, they'd say you were too big for your boots! You couldn't win.

Take Jeremiah for instance. He's one of those Bible characters known as a prophet. That doesn't mean he was your average reader of tea leaves or crystal ball gazer. What Jeremiah had was a sensitivity to people and events that let him see what the consequences of a certain line of action were likely to be – and a sensitivity to God, so that what he had to say had the ring of truth about it. Not that truth is what people always want to hear, which is why Jeremiah didn't much fancy being a prophet.

He was only a youngster, the son of a village priest, at a time when Palestine was split in two. Israel in the north was already occupied by Assyria, and Judah in the south was close to suffering the same fate. Now nobody likes a prophet of doom and gloom, but Jeremiah could see it coming a mile off. Someone, he thought, should warn the people.

If it's not the Assyrians it'll be the Babylonians. Sooner or later we'll be invaded; and he put it down, in his simple religious way to the wickedness of the people. They were a selfish bunch, smug, complacent, dishonest, unjust. If their enemies attacked and destroyed them, Jeremiah reckoned it was only God's way of showing them they couldn't be disloyal and get away with it.

But you can only tell people that sort of thing if they're in the frame of mind to admit they're in the wrong. Jeremiah guessed that the people of Judah were nothing like ready to confess their sins and mend their ways, so he didn't want the job. 'I'm too young,' he said, 'I don't know how to talk to people.'

Well, you know what people are like. Disasters happen to *other* people; and the people of Judah had a touching, though misplaced faith in the sanctity of the Great Temple in Jerusalem, their centre of worship. As long as the Temple still stood, they thought they were safe. 'Don't you believe it,' said Jeremiah, taking up the challenge at last.

And he was right. The Babylonians invaded, destroyed Jerusalem and the Temple with it, and carted off the inhabitants to Babylon as slaves, though not before the warnings of Jeremiah had been heard and ignored time and time again.

The people accused him of being unpatriotic, of demoralizing the armed forces. When he went to the trouble of writing his message down for the benefit of the king, the scroll was cut to pieces and hurled into the fire. They beat him, imprisoned him, and stuck him in a disused well to die of starvation. A foreigner came to his rescue. No one else wanted to know.

It was well said centuries later by Jesus of Nazareth that a prophet has no honour in his own country. A man of God like Jeremiah must have foreseen the opposition of his own people as readily as he saw the invasion of the Babylonians. You couldn't blame him for not wanting to do it. 'Too young,' he'd said, though he must have known in his heart that if he was called by God then the words would come, and the strength, to meet the demands of the job. 'Too young,' he said, but in the end, against great odds, he did what he believed God wanted him to do.

And every Christian knows that facing life's difficulties with the confidence that you've got God's backing is the surest way to maturity.

Going to Pot

The word that came to Jeremiah from the Lord: 'Arise and go down to the potter's house, and there you will hear my words.' So I went down to the potter's house, and there he was working at his wheel. And the vessel he was making of clay was spoiled in the potter's hand, and he reworked it into another vessel, as it seemed good to the potter to do (Jeremiah 18.1–4).

Amazing stuff, clay. It never ceases to amaze me that a soft and really rather messy substance is capable in skilled hands of becoming a thing of beauty. From earth to porcelain vase, it's a miracle of transformation.

I suppose you could play the miracle down and just call it modelling and baking, but it's still pretty remarkable. It responds to so many different ways of treating it. You can press it into shape with your bare hands, or press it into a plaster mould, or even pour it into a mould if you liquefy it first into a kind of thin grey custard. You can shape it on a potter's wheel, or roll it out like pastry and cut it with a knife.

Left to dry it soon becomes brittle and fragile, but even if you break it at that stage, you can mix it with water, reconstitute it and use it again. It's when you've baked it in a kiln at somewhere between 800 and 1200 Celsius that the change takes place which is irreversible. It becomes a kind of stone.

What Jeremiah the prophet saw when he visited the potter's workshop was an image that seemed to fit his own situation. The armies of Assyria were about to invade, and Jeremiah, in true prophetic tradition, blamed it all on the nation's capacity for wickedness. The imminent destruction of Jerusalem and the slaughter of its people was

God's punishment, he reckoned – or if you like, his way of demolishing and re-shaping a misshapen Israel.

That was twenty-five centuries ago. To me, the image says something different today. Working as I do with children, it's possible to think of them as a kind of soft clay, impressionable and open to the imprint on their young minds of attitudes, right or wrong, shaped by adult example. Just suppose, by mistreatment or neglect, their characters are misshapen, or their emotions warped, so that today's patterns of hatred, prejudice or maladjustment are baked into the attitudes of future generations. Something else Jeremiah said had to do with the sins of the fathers coming home to their children after them – what some people might call *original sin* passed on from one generation to another.

But Christians believe that God once took a hand in human affairs to re-shape them – taking human shape himself, in the body of a man called Jesus of Nazareth, whose totally unselfish life, whose compassion and commitment to others was second to none. Threatened by the sin of others, he responded, not with anger or violence, but with love and pity. He's the man to whom Christians look as the one in all history who, seeing the potential of one generation's foolishness to infect the next, was determined, at least in his own life, to stop it – not to pass it on. It destroyed him. His enemies crucified him. But the story of his coming to life again, embodies the Christian hope that God can take a life, ruined by its own sin, or the sin of others, and remake it.

Winds of Change

The hand of the Lord was upon me, and he brought me out by the Spirit of the Lord and set me down in the midst of the valley; it was full of bones. And he led me round among them; and behold there were very many upon the valley; and lo, they were very dry. And he said to me, 'Son of man, can these bones live?'

Then he said to me, 'Prophesy to the breath, prophesy, son of man, and say to the breath, 'Thus says the Lord God, "Come from the four winds O breath and breathe upon these slain that they may live" ' (Ezekiel 37.1–3, 9).

You wouldn't have thought there was any hope of even a breath of wind, the day we all trooped down to Hemsby beach with the picnic things and the kite – four grown-ups and five children in a fit of determined lunacy to make the best of a washed-out holiday. It was Thursday already, and it hadn't stopped raining since Sunday. We'd done the amusements and the castles and museums, and every other kind of indoor pastime you can think of but, after all, when you go to the seaside for a holiday, you reckon to go to the beach, sunbathe, swim, doze, build sandcastles with the kids, fly a kite.

Ah yes, the kite. There we sat, huddled amongst the sand dunes in our plastic macs, surrounded by a thick grey blanket of sea mist, and somebody said, 'Let's see if we can get the kite up.' 'But there isn't any wind!'

Well, you wouldn't have thought so, but we put the old box kite together, tossed it rather pessimistically into the air . . . and it *flew*! It rose into the mist and vanished from sight. I remember letting out yard after yard of string, and feeling the strong pull of the kite I

couldn't even see, and the drops of moisture running down the string like wet beads into my fingers. Beyond the mist, up there somewhere, there was wind – moving air, the life-giving breath, the invisible power.

It's easy to see why an ancient Bible prophet like Ezekiel would use the wind to represent the spirit of God breathing life into a defeated and demoralized nation. In his day – round about 580 BC, Jerusalem had been destroyed by the armies of Babylon, and those who weren't killed in the fighting were taken to Babylon as prisoners of war. Homesick and without hope, by the rivers of Babylon – as one of the psalms and a later pop-song put it – they sat down and wept when they remembered Zion. Zion was Jerusalem. Home.

After all, their folk history assured them they were God's chosen people. Yet there they were, prisoners and slaves in a foreign land. But the prophet Ezekiel had a vision. I guess he'd once stood in a valley where the remnants of the bodies killed in battle lay in the dust, but in his mind's eye he saw the dry bones miraculously covered in sinew, muscle and skin. Then from the four winds came the breath that put new life into them. Israel reborn!

Well it took fifty years or so, until Cyrus king of Persia, attacked and defeated the Babylonians and let the Jews go. There's more than a hint in this story of the same kind of optimism Christians find in the story of Jesus Christ dying and coming to life again. People who trust God have a way of bouncing back. They're not prepared to be defeated by pain, hardship or tragedy, but use it to good account, to fashion strong character and shape convictions – always provided they hold on with sufficient faith to keep them from bitterness and resentment.

For the world needs those who can face great odds with courage and cheerfulness. They're not the victims of some divine whim, but through them, God can let loose into the world the invisible power, the winds of change that Christians call the Holy Spirit, and for all who are influenced by it, life begins again.

The Writing on the Wall

Immediately the fingers of a man's hand appeared and wrote on the plaster of the wall of the king's palace, opposite the lampstand; and the king saw the hand as it wrote. Then the king's colour changed, and his thoughts alarmed him; his limbs gave way, and his knees knocked together.

'Then from his presence the hand was sent, and this writing was inscribed: MENE, MENE, TEKEL and PARSIN. This is the interpretation of the matter: MENE, God has numbered the days of your kingdom and brought it to an end; TEKEL, you have been weighed in the balances and found wanting; PERES, your kingdom is divided and given to the Medes and the Persians' (Daniel 5.5–6, 24–28).

On the dull wall of the subway under the bypass on the edge of town Stephen Robert Kipling wrote his name. Well – sort of. He was known to his mates as *Kipper*. It was this well-known nickname, with the aid of an aerosol can of red paint, and in letters some twelve inches high, that he added to the random collection of scrawls and legends in a rainbow of colours which, truth to tell, actually livened up a rather drab concrete tunnel. But, consciously or unconsciously, *Kipper*, adding his signature to the works of a dozen or more unlicensed artists, had effectively sealed his fate.

For the trouble was, *Kipper* had made his mark once too often. Recognition of any other sort eluding him, he'd sought it through minor acts of crime and violence. The local police knew *Kipper* well. Any excuse would have done. They translated his foot-high letters as criminal damage and arrested him on the steps of the picture-house. For *Kipper* – literally – the writing had been on the wall, a doom-laden phrase handed down to us from the Bible's Book of Daniel. Fate's victim there, however, was a king called Belshazzar; though what you have to understand is that the story is not about him at all. Let me explain.

The Book of Daniel is a kind of religious and political tract written to give heart to a persecuted people. The Jews were having a bad time under the rule and whim of a Syrian king. I suppose if you're saddled with a name like Antiochus (the Fourth) Epiphanes, you'd want to take it out on somebody. If it hadn't been the Jews I dare say it would have been somebody else. He was greedy for power and empire, and a nasty piece of work all together. Just for kicks, he knocked down the walls of Jerusalem, put up heathen statues in the most sacred place in the Temple, burned the Jews' holy books, and forced them to do what no self-respecting Jew would even contemplate; he made them eat roast pork!

It might be funny if it weren't so tragically true. Insult added to injury, oppression and humiliation. But to make public protest would have been suicidal. Dissidents were apt to disappear mysteriously. They ended up in prison, or dead. So the book of Daniel wasn't even written by Daniel. That's the name of an ancient hero which the real author borrowed to save his own skin. And he set the story too, in ancient times, when Israel had been conquered by Babylon, and the Babylonian king was Belshazzar. Jews reading the story would know better. It was meant for their own times. For Belshazzar, read Antiochus. And then read on.

The king was throwing a party for the aristocracy, a grand affair with over a thousand guests; and with the cruel mockery that those who think themselves superior often excel at, they were swilling down the wine from gold and silver vessels they'd looted from the temple; people with no religion and no sensitivity either. But who'd want to tell them so?

The funny thing about graffiti is the way you never see who puts it there. It just appears – as it did at Belshazzar's Feast. A phantom hand inscribed this cryptic message on the wall:

MENE, MENE, TEKEL and PARSIN

The king was terrified; his wise men were mystified. Only God's spokesman Daniel could break the code – *heavyweight, pennyweight and half-measure*, or in old money, *a pound, a penny and a ten bob*

מצא מצא
הקל
ופרמין

note – or something like that; at any rate, a jolly jingle to do with weights and coins and what a person might be worth. It took on a new and sinister meaning.

The king wasn't worth much. God had weighed him and found him short measure. He might have had power and position, but he'd soon discover how those who put themselves on a pedestal are prone to come down to earth with a crash. The higher they climb the further they fall, and those who play God fall furthest.

The advantage of history is that you can see whether those who looked likely to come to a bad end actually did. So what about Antiochus (the Fourth) Epiphanes? Went stark, staring mad, and died of a mysterious disease. The *chicken and egg* sort of question is whether it was power and the abuse of power which drove him mad, or like most tyrannical dictators, was he mad to start with?

All you can say is that the Book of Daniel was right to bid the Jews take heart. It was saying: 'This hardship can't last forever. Don't lose your grip on God. He'll see you through.' I suppose nobody would have blamed them if they'd said, 'That's all very well, but in dark days like these, life's too dear and words of comfort and encouragement come too cheap and easy.' Anyone might be tempted to talk like that. Even a Christian. But he might just look at it differently. The Book of Daniel is the book in which the hero survives a night in a den of ravenous lions, and three of his mates – Shadrach, Meshach, and Abed-nego – survive a terrible ordeal by fire. What a Christian might see at once is the parallel with the death and survival of Jesus Christ. The truth he stood for – that the worth of humanity is measured, not in status or wealth, but in personal endeavour, integrity, faith and compassion for those in need – is a truth that never dies; and those who hold to it are survivors, even if they choose to die for it.

Now there's a contradiction. Or is it? Christians put their faith in the possibility that God's promise of eternal life means exchanging one way of living for another, so they might as well take the risk, stand firm, and *Dare* – as the old song puts it – *to be a Daniel*. To know that what you stand for is worth much more to God than money or position is to be weighed in the balance, and to find, unlike Belshazzar or Antiochus, that you carry all the weight you need.

Scenes From a Marriage

And the Lord said to me, 'Go again, love a woman who is beloved of a paramour and is an adulteress; even as the Lord loves the people of Israel though they turn to other gods and love cakes of raisins.' So I bought her for fifteen shekels of silver and a homer and a lethech of barley. And I said to her, 'You must dwell as mine for many days; you shall not play the harlot, or belong to another man; so will I also be to you.' For the children of Israel shall dwell many days without king or prince, without sacrifice or pillar, without ephod or teraphim. Afterward the children of Israel shall return and seek the Lord their God, and David their king; and they shall come in fear to the Lord and to his goodness in the latter days (Hosea 3.1–5).

It wasn't a peace-offering, honestly it wasn't. The fact that we'd disagreed and I'd left the house and slammed the car door, and driven as if on automatic pilot towards Great Yarmouth had nothing to do with it. Well . . . maybe I protest too much. From a phone box by the Chinese Take-away I rang my wife at home.

'It's me,' I said.
'I thought it might be,' she said.
'I thought I'd bring a meal home. I'm just by the Chinese . . .'
'Well . . .' she answered, a little bit surprised and uncertain,
' . . . all right.'

I can't even remember what we'd quarrelled about. The children probably. Whatever it was, we'd both needed our own space and time to put things in perspective and discover that respect for each other's independence often enhanced our coming together again.

Arriving home with the fried rice and the sweet and sour pork in its little brown carrier bag, confirmed it. In a strange way the disagreement was evidence that at the heart of our relationship were things that mattered sufficiently to both of us to be worth the pain of argument. It was only the details we argued about, the day to day working out of basic principles on which there had always been some measure of agreement, or else perhaps we should never have married in the first place.

Quarrels, like flotsam and jetsam on the surface of living, need do no harm if deep beneath the waves in the love, understanding and readiness to sort things out together, is the security which quarrels may threaten to destroy, but with God's help may serve to strengthen.

Now if that all sounds a bit smug, it's because the quarrel was twelve years ago, since when the children have grown up and departed to live their own lives, and at this distance the pain of the struggle towards independence – for them *and* us – seems a lot less agonizing than it did at the time; and with the luxury of hindsight I can take time to reflect on the lessons I've learned – or failed to learn – from married life.

One thing is plain: if marriages are made in heaven, the evidence of heaven's influence isn't always clear to see. Perhaps, after all, they're made on earth and the heaven or hell of them is what we create for ourselves. What are you to make, for instance, of a marriage in the Bible which, if you take the Bible at its word, was ordered to take place by God himself but which, to anyone with an atom of common sense was doomed to failure from the word *go*.

The marriage was that of Hosea the prophet to Gomer the prostitute. The way the Bible tells it, it looks as though he knew she was a bad lot before he married her, and ought to have had more sense. Having borne him three children, she cleared off back to her old ways again. Or did she? Maybe it's just the way Hosea tells it, after the custom of his day, looking back and translating the tragedy of his experience in terms of a God whom, he believed, had everything mapped out for him from the beginning.

No one would see it that way these days. It relieves us of any responsibility for our own actions – *Don't blame me, God said I was to do it!* – and gives us no part to play in our own destinies.

My guess would be that Hosea, deeply in love and innocent of any crisis looming in his marriage, suddenly found himself discarded by a wife who'd grown tired of him and the kids, and was desperate for something a bit more exciting. Whether she cared what she'd done is anyone's guess. For Hosea the wrench was grievous, and brought it home to him just how much he loved her. He was heart-broken, and he didn't care how much she'd hurt him; he wanted her back.

While all this was happening, there was something of a national crisis on. Now the gift of a prophet lay in his sensitivity to the way things looked to be going, both religious and political; and the way it looked to Hosea was that his fellow countrymen were any day now likely to be attacked by the armies of Assyria. The reason was that the king of Assyria had a mind to conquer Egypt and little places like Syria, Israel and Judah just happened to be *en route*.

For a man of God in Hosea's day, however, that wasn't reason enough. Hosea's view took Assyria's invasion to be a just punishment for Israel's wickedness. The prophet was appalled at the extent of crime and violence. Even the priesthood was corrupt, allowing the people to play fast and loose with God's affections, worshipping him one moment, bowing down to idols the next.

The parallel was inescapable. Hosea had married a harlot wife. God was married to a harlot nation. Not only was Israel morally and spiritually in ruins but, the way Hosea saw it, when she ought to have sought God's help in the face of this imminent Assyrian invasion, she hankered instead for alliances with Syria and Egypt – in his view highly adulterous affairs.

It's powerful stuff, conveying through the pain of a husband rejected and humiliated by a heartless woman, something of the agony of a cry from the heart of God himself for a people he loved in spite of their unfaithfulness. 'I love you,' says God. 'Won't you say you love me too?'

It was a gesture of forgiveness, and an insight by Hosea into the character of God which was seven hundred years before its time. Christians believe that Jesus Christ was the human shape of God in whom it was made plain through parable, healing ministry, devotion, death and resurrection that God is ready to bear the hurt of his people's stupidity, cruelty, greed and spite. For one of the reasons people go off the rails into prostitution, crime or anything else, is that they have themselves at some time been rejected or abused, finding no one prepared to love them with all the love they need to make them feel secure.

God knows this and, I would think, expects Christians to know it too and respond accordingly, extending most love, not to those who will immediately love them back, but to those who because they stand in most need of loving, are often the most difficult to love.

A Hard Day's Night

And I will give portents in the heavens and on earth, blood and fire, and columns of smoke. The sun shall be turned to darkness, and the moon to blood, before the great and terrible day of the Lord comes. And it shall come to pass that all who call upon the name of the Lord shall be delivered; for in Mount Zion and in Jerusalem there shall be those who escape, as the Lord has said, and among the survivors shall be those whom the Lord calls (Joel 2.30–32).

I can see my mother now, standing on the kitchen doorstep, breadknife in one hand, half a loaf in the other, stopped in the middle of preparing tea, to gaze across the fields at the back of the house and declare, 'Looks black over Bill's mother's.' Not that Bill's mother had anything to do with it. Storm clouds are a natural phenomenon that need no assistance from Bill's mother or anyone else to gather in the great masses that darken the sky and threaten a downpour. It was simply my mother's usual phrase for describing the signs in the sky that prompted her gloomy forecast.

Standing on the same back step early one summer evening, she'd seen another sign – a column, steadily growing into a wide pall of black smoke and several shades of grey, that was surely a sign of fire and destruction. It was. Next morning, on my way to school I passed the blackened ruins of St. Barnabas' Church where two boys had gone in and made a little bonfire of hymn books that had soon become an uncontrollable inferno.

Signs in the sky don't necessarily have to be supernatural ones, though if a prophet has a gift for poetry as well, the way he says things can sometimes give the impression of supernatural intervention. If you happen, like Joel for instance, to be of a literary and prophetic

turn of mind, it can take very little to trigger off a piece of creative writing, although if the incident happens to be a dramatic one, so much the better.

What started Joel off was a plague of locusts, those fierce relations of the grasshopper with such terrible appetites they can strip a field of crops in seconds. An army of them on the move, their approach blotting out the sun and darkening the sky, would strike fear into the heart of any farmer. He'd see, if not his whole life exactly flashing before him, a year's toil, a year's harvest, and next year's seed devoured in an instant – past, present and future consumed in one fell swoop.

And it's past, present and future that Joel's prophecy is really about. At the heart of his strange vision was a religious tradition that looked forward to a day when everything in the world that was evil and unjust would be swept away. God would arrive, putting it all right, destroying the wicked and saving the good. And how else would God come but with demonstrations of his greatness and power – an eclipse of the sun, the eruption of a volcano. And because – in Joel's view – he had always in the past used human agencies to punish the nation for its sins, God's judgment would include many battles. The signs of his coming would be seen in the columns of smoke that rose from the burning shells of ruined cities, and the pools of wasted blood on the battlefields.

Sometimes I get Jehovah's Witnesses on my doorstep, pointing in their Bibles to words like those of Joel, and insisting that *any day now* the day of the Lord and the end of the world is going to come and God's harsh judgment with it; and they back up their belief with stories from the newspapers: earthquakes in South America, killings in Northern Ireland, the rising tide of crime and violence, the arms race, the Soviet threat and – almost as though history were not so much repeating itself as continuing a long-running saga – wars and rumours of wars in the Middle East. When I've pointed out to the Jehovah's Witnesses that they've been saying the day of the Lord and the end of the world is coming *any day now* for at least a hundred years, and I've finally managed to say goodbye and close the door, I sometimes think they've got it right and wrong at the same time.

When I think about the conflicts in several parts of the world in which people are killing each other with all sorts of ingenious weaponry, and laying waste cities they once built with the same ingenuity, I think perhaps the day of the Lord is already with us. Not some twenty-four-hour job. We're talking about God's time. But people are fighting for what they believe is right. They've done so since time began, and signs of conflict litter the pages of history. But for all we know, the records of centuries occupy the space of just one small entry in the diary of God for *one day*.

And the death and destruction we dare to call his judgment, he looks upon with love, compassion and, above all, patience, knowing that if he waits long enough, what we refuse to be *told*, we will by the end of the day, have learned at last for ourselves, and it will make *his day* complete.

Straight and True

. . . behold, the Lord was standing beside a wall built with a plumb line, with a plumb line in his hand. And the Lord said to me, 'Amos, what do you see?' And I said, 'A plumb line.' Then the Lord said, 'Behold, I am setting a plumb line in the midst of my people Israel; I will never again pass by them; the high places of Isaac shall be made desolate, and the sanctuaries of Israel shall be laid waste, and I will rise against the house of Jeroboam with the sword' (Amos 7.7–9).

Only a do-it-yourself enthusiast with many years experience will remember a machine, now long obsolete, which trimmed the edges of wallpaper in the days when it came with protective margins half an inch wide on each side. Until the advent of this wonderful machine, you tackled the edges almost warily with a pair of scissors, a steady hand and a good eye. If, when I wielded the scissors less than accurately and the pieces of paper as I hung them, failed to line up neatly, I had only myself to blame; but, when they'd been machine-trimmed in the shop, I immediately had an excuse – 'Look at it, they didn't trim it straight!' It's been a family motto ever since.

As a matter of fact, even before the machine, I could find an excuse. It was the walls that weren't straight then, or the corners that were out of true; no, it was the skirting boards that weren't level. Always there was something. I mean, how could it possibly be *me?*

Professional decorators, I knew, used a plumb line to get at least the first piece hanging straight. The rest hung true from that one, but even today, ignoring expert know-how, I tend to trust my own unaided judgment, and I guess it serves me right if the job isn't as well done as it might be. But it's too much fuss getting things straight. It takes so long, and nothing annoys me more than people with an obsession for perfection who spend hours and hours, fiddling about with a job until they are absolutely satisfied with it. I just haven't got that sort of patience. I want the job done and finished with.

Mind you, hanging wallpaper is one thing. Living is another. I get irritated just the same if people who think they know what's right and wrong start telling me what I ought to do. Who do they think they are, anyway? The way they go on about sex and violence on TV and pretend to know the right decision on every moral issue a man or woman has to face, you'd think they had a hot-line to God, and I'd guess I'm not alone in finding their attitude obnoxious. And I dare say that trying to lay down hard and fast rules about living, and criticizing those who don't come up to scratch provoked as much irritation in the days of Amos the sheep-farmer, as it does now.

Who, for goodness' sake, was a simple sheep farmer, to think he could set himself up as a prophet and tell a whole nation where he thought they were going wrong? Down on the building site one day, he saw the builder using a plumb line to check if a wall was upright, and it gave him an idea. A plumb line was just what God needed to see if his people were true. In Amos' view they were anything but. Round about 760 BC society, according to Amos was corrupt. Judges took bribes, shopkeepers gave short measure. The sick, the widow and the homeless were mistreated and neglected. The rich got richer and the poor got poorer.

'So cut it out!' says Amos, 'This is no way to carry on. God wouldn't approve.' And in his simple religious way he made an equation between the wickedness of the people and the threat of invasion by Babylon. If you sinned, Amos reckoned, there was a price to pay, and this would be it. But when these hard-hitting home truths appeared to be critical of king and government he'd clearly gone too far. One of the king's loyal subjects, a priest called Amaziah, told tales on Amos, and returned from the king to deliver a message couched, of course, in language appropriate to his calling and the times in which he spoke, but plainly saying to Amos – 'Get lost!'

But lone voices, like today's moral minorities, have a habit of holding on once they've got their teeth into what they believe is a righteous cause. And maybe it's just as well. Who knows how far we'd go astray if their teeth didn't nip the flesh of our consciences every so often?

The only trouble with Amos was . . . he was right!

Deep Down

Now the word of the Lord came to Jonah the son of Amittai, saying, 'Arise, go to Nineveh, that great city, and cry against it; for their wickedness has come up before me.' But Jonah rose to flee to Tarshish from the presence of the Lord (Jonah 1.1–3).

There's nothing worse than being *told*. There's a built-in resistance in all of us, I reckon, to being told what we can do and what we can't. When you're a youngster it's worse: 'You change those trousers before you go out, my lad, and stay away from that river. What's that? . . . You'll *do* as you're *told!*'

To a lad with an ounce of adventure in him, 'You stay out of that tree' would be enough to make him. . . . well . . . climb a tree! Though, sometimes it's not so much a sense of adventure as a spirit of stubbornness, and that's as common in grown-ups as it is in children. Take Jonah for instance, he was stubborn. 'Get up,' said God, 'and go to that great city Nineveh and pronounce its doom. Its shameful wickedness has been reported to me.' But Jonah didn't want to go. It wasn't just a matter of not wanting to be bothered. There was a whole mixed bag of emotions working away inside him from racial prejudice to fear for his own life, not to mention the thought that if you had a good idea – in this instance a belief in a personal God – it was something you kept to yourself.

The story is set in a time nearly eight hundred years before Christ, when the people of Israel thought God was their own private property and wouldn't want anything to do with the foreigners who lived across the border. In fact, they thought if you travelled far enough you'd be out of God's reach all together.

Now the city that Jonah had been ordered to go to – Nineveh – was the capital of Assyria, and the Assyrians were not only foreigners – a heathen lot – but they were also sworn and long-term enemies of Israel. No wonder Jonah didn't want to go there. Ignorance and self-interest make cowards of us all. So instead of setting out for Nineveh, Jonah took to his heels in the opposite direction – or rather, took to sea, to sail as far away from God as possible.

It's the story you'll know as *Jonah and the Whale*, though the Bible says nothing about a whale, only a great fish. No matter. A storm blew up and the ship's crew, looking for someone to blame for it, tossed up, or threw dice – something like that – and it was Jonah, so they threw him overboard. And that's how he came to get swallowed by a fish that only spewed him up again so that, having had a not-so-gentle warning, he'd now go and do as he'd been told.

So he did. He made his way to Nineveh and pronounced its ruin unless the people mended their wicked ways. Then he sat back to see what God would do. And an amazing thing happened. The words of Jonah reached the ears of the king who issued a proclamation:

By order of the king and his ministers, a time of fasting is announced, when neither man nor beast shall eat or drink, but they shall put on sackcloth and pray with all their hearts to almighty God. Let everyone turn from his evil ways and acts of violence.

'Who knows?' the king said, 'Perhaps God will change his mind and the city will be saved.' And he did. And it was. And Jonah was *furious*!

He'd wanted retribution, but he'd got it all wrong; and the author of the story only wrote it because he believed the people of Israel had got it all wrong too. Their vision of God was much too small and needed to grow. It was another eight hundred years before Jesus of Nazareth came and spelled out the bigness of God, and even though nearly two thousand years have passed since then, it's still a temptation to think that some people are inferior – because they're foreign, because they hold different opinions, or earn less than we do, or do a job we think is less important – the list is probably endless. And as long as it is, it's a sure sign that our own vision of God still has an awful lot of growing to do.

Up the Airy Mountain

It shall come to pass in the latter days that the mountain of the house of the Lord shall be established as the highest of the mountains, and shall be raised up above the hills; and peoples shall flow to it, and many nations shall come and say: 'Come, let us go up to the mountain of the Lord, to the house of the God of Jacob; that he may teach us his ways and we may walk in his paths' (Micah 4.1–2).

But you, O Bethlehem Ephrathah, who are little to be among the clans of Judah, from you shall come forth for me one who is to be ruler in Israel, whose origin is from of old, from ancient days (Micah 5.2).

The nearest thing to a mountain I've ever climbed is Snowdon. Even then, I have to admit, I climbed it by car, urging it up ever steeper, narrower and twistier roads until we were as near as we could get, only to find the mountain top hidden by thick cloud. We sat in the car, eating our damp packed lunches, the landscape we had hoped to admire from a great height lost amongst layers of clinging wet mist.

It didn't diminish my fascination with high places. Once when I was small my mother, thinking I was lost, called my name and missed a heart-beat or two when I answered from the top of a tree a hundred feet or so above her head. Matlock's cable-car ride to Abraham's Heights and the topmost platform of the Eiffel Tower have satisfied the same desire.

It's not just a case of distance lending enchantment to the view. There's something to be said for the sheer exhilaration of climbing high. I can well understand the lure of Everest's summit. All the same, details of the landscape which may well be ugly close to – electricity

pylons and eyesores dreamed up in an architect's nightmare – become less intrusive in the wider panorama of the view from on high.

I dare say it's why Micah, that old Bible prophet, invited the Jews of his day – 700 BC or so – to join him in their imaginations to climb the mountain of the Lord. Mind you, like so many visions, his mountain-top view of the world had its roots in reality. The temple at Jerusalem, which was for Jews the very centre of their faith, was built on the hill they called Mount Zion. From here perhaps, though only perhaps, they could be helped to see the world through God's eyes, for Micah sensed that even tiny features of the landscape – villages lost in the distance, or hidden by hills or trees – still belonged to the same world as Mount Zion, a world which in fact wouldn't be complete without them. A small town like Bethlehem, for instance, Micah reckoned was capable of playing an important part in God's plans – an idea seized upon later, of course, when Jesus happened to be born there, as if Micah had known it was going to happen.

Who knows? What Micah was getting at was *Small is Beautiful*. The heady air of ritual and worship on Mount Zion was all very well, but useless unless it made some difference to the little man in the street, the poor man very often, evicted from his farmland, trampled on by the rich and powerful, and robbed by priests and prophets who expected fat fees for their services. These were only a few of the blots on Micah's human landscape. Never mind the mountain-top experience, Micah was saying; all God really wants is for people to play fair, show each other mercy, and not hold inflated opinions of themselves:

> *He has showed you, O man what is good; and what does the Lord require of you but to do justice, and to love kindness, and to walk humbly with your God? (Micah 6.8)*

My wife doesn't like heights. They make her giddy and give her a terrible feeling of insecurity. In Paris she ventured as far as the first floor of the Eiffel Tower and left me to scale the dizzier heights – by means of the lift! – but on my own. She prefers to keep her feet on the ground.

When all's said and done, there's nothing much to do from a high vantage point except admire the view, let it take your breath away, and then perhaps realize you'll need all the breath you've got to make the journey down again. You can kid yourself that you're nearer to God up there, but Christians have come to believe, from reading their

New Testaments and thinking about the healing, teaching, courage and self-sacrifice of Jesus of Nazareth, that in him God himself came down to earth, and that to serve God properly and bring about the justice and peace that Micah cried out for, we long for, and God plans, is a down-to-earth job for down-to-earth people.

Streets Ahead

Thus says the Lord of hosts: Old men and old women shall again sit in the streets of Jerusalem, each with staff in hand for very age. And the streets of the city shall be full of boys and girls playing in its streets (Zechariah 8.4–5).

Nobody worried that we played in the streets, even after dark. A gas lamp stood not far from the house where I lived as a boy, and traffic was scarce. I remember, just once, when I left the pavement on one side and headed at great speed for the other, colliding with a girl on a bike. But even bikes were few and far between. The street was our playground, safe and close to home.

We played *tip-cat*, a game that involved a small length of wood, pointed at both ends being leant against the kerb and given a sharp clout with a two-foot rod so that it spun into the air. Then you gave it another whack that sent it way down the street while you ran like blazes, scoring runs until the others fetched it back again. And there were several versions of *ticky*. One of us was *it* and had to catch one of the others who then became *it*, and so it went on until we grew tired of it. There was *French ticky* where you held on to the part of the body where the person who'd been *it* had touched you, and you couldn't release your hold until you'd touched somebody else. It meant prancing about, trying to catch the others, in some pretty contorted positions. There was *ticky off-ground*, where the boy or girl who was *it* couldn't touch you if you weren't actually standing on the road or pavement. Half way up a fence or lamp post, or standing on a step was sanctuary. Manhole covers, I remember, didn't count.

If I didn't quite so vividly remember the girl on the bike, limping off into the dark, pushing the bike because she was clearly too hurt

and shocked to get back on again, it would be easy to think that my childhood was just one long, warm, idyllic summer evening under the yellow glow of the street lamp with cries of laughter echoing from friends and playmates, and never a mother coming to the front door to shout, 'Come on in, you. It's way past your bedtime!'

Happy dreams!

I can't help thinking that Zechariah was indulging in a little nostalgia when he had a vision of children playing happily in the streets of Jerusalem. He saw the old folks too, sitting in the streets. The ones I remember hardly did that, but the summer evenings did bring them out to lean on the front gate and pass the time of day with neighbours and passers-by in good-natured banter and idle gossip.

Happy days!

And for Zechariah it was almost a case of *Happy Days are Here Again.* His fellow countrymen, the Jews, had been through some hard times. They'd seen their city reduced to ruins by the Babylonian armies, their holy temple destroyed and most of the citizens, if they hadn't died in the fighting, had been marched off, many of them to spend the rest of their lives as prisoners of war in Babylon. But, by the time Zechariah was writing – 536 BC or thereabouts – Babylon itself had been conquered by Persia, and the Persian Emperor had let the Jews go, to return home and rebuild their homes and lives again.

So they had; but they needed no end of encouragement to start work, so Zechariah tried to rouse a bit of enthusiasm by offering them this vision of city streets where young and old alike would be able to live without fear. The good old days were on the way back!

I can't say how old Zechariah might have been. This dream of his sounds a little bit like the idealism of youth, but perhaps rather more like the longings of an old man for days rose-tinted by the passage of time and long past resurrection. Both harmless enough, I suppose, were it not for the rather more peculiar visions he had which, for me, have sinister undertones.

He sees, for instance, a flying scroll – a lengthy document some thirty feet long and fifteen feet wide that appears to set out the penalties for theft and perjury. The flying element, I'd guess is to make sure it was equipped to reach the ears of everyone. Then he had a vision of four men in horse-drawn chariots patrolling the four corners of the earth and keeping the peace. It gives me the creeps. Is this ancient prophet promoting the notion, I wonder, that the peace and safety of city streets that he dreams of, have to be secured by a strict enforcement of law and order, stiffer penalties for crime and police-state surveillance?

I don't know if I'm reading too much between the lines. Maybe Zechariah is writing tongue-in-cheek, and his strange word-pictures are painted in a way that's meant to disguise his real intention – a timely warning. If people don't learn for themselves the self-discipline that helps them treat other people with love and respect, then those in power – the money-makers and the politicians – will try to secure it by restrictive laws and oppression, and mostly for the sake of their own ambition. So watch out.

One of the odd things about the Bible is how you can often translate what it says to suit yourself and yet, however you translate it, you end up with the same truth. No matter how you look at it, Zechariah's message is the old truth that you can't have freedom without responsibility. The only question then is: Do you need someone else to impose responsibility upon you, or can you be responsible for yourself?

The question is the same one that people are asking when they see the mess the world is in and want to know why God doesn't step in and *do* something. 'Oh, but he *did!*' says the Christian, 'Jesus of Nazareth was his way of stepping in; but not to stop the rot, and certainly not to give the impression that if we could only get back to the good old days the world would be all sweetness and light. What this God in human shape made plain was that the world's trouble is a responsibility that has to be borne by everybody. If not, then the innocent get hurt, and if the whole world opts out, then the one remaining good, blameless man has to bear the responsibility, and the suffering, all alone.'

Who'd be a Christian, if trying to be like Jesus means such terrible responsibility? Who'd be a Christian if taking responsibility for ourselves means taking responsibility for other people too, and not minding if we get hurt sometimes? The Christian believes the risk is worth taking.

When we used to play in the street, the games sometimes ended in quarrelling and tears when somebody broke or changed the rules. Next day, as is the way more with children than with grown-ups, we'd be there again, playing as if the quarrels of the day before had never happened. A new beginning. The story of Jesus doesn't end with his death, nor even with his resurrection. It's a continuing series of new beginnings which the freedom to bear other people's stupidity and pain makes possible.

You can of course choose not to get involved. That's what freedom's all about. But at least if you accept the responsibility of choosing – whether you opt for good or evil – it makes you worth something. You're *somebody*. So who wants a God who keeps us in order with strict laws and an army of Thought Police who make it impossible for us to break them? Nobody wants to be a nobody, and I'm quite sure God knows it.

Mother Mary

In the sixth month the angel Gabriel was sent from God to the city of Galilee named Nazareth, to a virgin betrothed to a man whose name was Joseph, of the house of David; and the virgin's name was Mary (Luke 1.26–27).

I'd see her as more of a Chloe Patrick really. The Marys I've known have all been a bit limp and refined, not unlike the romantic portraits you see of Mother Mary – the Botticelli look, much too demure and saintly to have ever suffered the harassment of bringing up a family.

No. Chloe Patrick's more the picture. I used to know Chloe, though where she got a name like that I can't think. She came from such an ordinary family, though maybe it wasn't so ordinary if I think about it. The children used to come to Sunday School . . . Lenny, Alice, Susan, Michael, George, Steve, Deborah and Gloria. With Mum and Dad there were ten. How they all got into a small three-bedroomed council house I can't imagine. I guess they all slept somewhere, and pretty tightly packed!

I remember the living room, stacked high with jumble-sale clothes, and a high old-fashioned pram standing in a space under the stairs. Poor old Chloe, I used to think. All those mouths to feed and bodies to clothe. No wonder she had a job to make ends meet and looked more like fifty-two than thirty-two. A social worker called one day and hinted to Dad that eight kids was more than enough and shouldn't he take some preventive measures. 'You mind your own damned business,' he said, and that was that, so it wasn't long before Chloe was pregnant with number nine.

We met her one day, my wife and I, wheeling the new arrival in the big black pram across the local playing field. I'm not sure what we said. We admired the baby, but we must have managed to suggest that it was something of a burden for Chloe to have to cope with another one. She put us to shame, with a phrase like a piece of ancient wisdom her family had probably handed down for generations. 'I know,' she said, 'but they allus bring love with 'em, don't they?'

Good old Chloe! What we'd seen as another body to feed and wash and put to bed, and drive her to distraction on wet Bank Holidays she saw, if not entirely as an angel, at least as something that had come with love and wanted loving.

So what about Mary's angel?

> *And he came to her and said, 'Hail, O favoured one, the Lord is with you!' But she was greatly troubled at the saying, and considered in her mind what sort of greeting this might be.*
> *And the angel said to her, 'Do not be afraid, Mary, for you have found favour with God. And behold, you will conceive in your womb and bear a son, and you shall call his name Jesus (Luke 1.28–31).*

The appearance of an angel is one of the ways the Bible has of saying that God's making a special announcement. After all, when Luke got round to writing this story, he already knew the kind of child Mary had given birth to – how Jesus of Nazareth had grown up, left home, left a good job, done three years teaching, preaching and healing; how he'd been killed by his enemies, and left the world, except that his rising again from the dead had secured him a permanent place in the hearts and minds of those who named themselves after him – the Christians.

So Luke could see how Mary's pregnancy had been something out of this world. And never mind angels! For Mary I'd think missed periods and morning sickness were signs enough. God doesn't always have to resort to the supernatural to make it plain you've a special part to play in his scheme of things. And it doesn't surprise me that for some Christians Mary has become the symbol of perfect motherhood.

Somewhere I came across the idea that the role of a mother could easily be likened to the work of Jesus. Just imagine a mother preparing the toast and the Ready Brek – it's Jesus feeding the multitude; or a mother cuddling a child that's fallen over, sticking on a plaster and kissing it better – it's Jesus healing the sick: or the mother clearing

up someone else's mess, or quietly (or sometimes not so quietly!) absorbing the anger and ingratitude of the teenager striving so hard for independence he rejects all advice and resents criticism – it's Jesus forgiving his enemies. And when she lies in bed past midnight wondering if her daughter will ever come home from the disco, or whether her son has come off his motorbike and is lying mangled in a ditch somewhere – it's Jesus suffering for those he loves.

These cares and anxieties are not, of course, entirely the concern of the mother. These days her traditional role is increasingly shared by the father. What parents are entrusted with is the care of the future, the nourishing of the world's human potential. It calls often for the patience of God himself – or even *her*self – the need to go on loving his children in spite of them.

Called to such high service, no wonder Mary was both honoured and troubled.

Table Talk

Now on the first day of Unleavened Bread, the disciples came to Jesus, saying, 'Where will you have us prepare for you to eat the passover?' He said, 'Go into the city to such a one, and say to him, "The Teacher says, My time is at hand; I will keep the passover at your house with my disciples." ' And the disciples did as Jesus directed them, and they prepared the passover (Matthew 26.17–19).

It was going to be a treat for the whole family; a day in London and a meal in a restaurant. Everybody else had brought packed lunches, but just for once we thought we'd be different. Treat ourselves. But we hadn't allowed for the traffic down the Mile End Road. We'd started from Norfolk at 7.30 in the morning. By the time we got to the City it was nearly one o'clock, so it was skates on to find somewhere to eat. We were getting pretty hungry. As the coach drew away, we headed for the nearest restaurant and in we went. If we'd had any sense we'd have come straight out again.

There was a musty smell as if the carpets hadn't been hoovered in years, and we couldn't find a table that wasn't in a draught. Then, when the meal eventually came, it was cold, half-cooked and tasteless. I felt so let down. What had promised to be a great occasion we'd all been looking forward to, turned out to be a real disappointment, though I'd guess it was nothing compared to the disappointment of a group of friends who once met to celebrate a great anniversary.

If I tell you that the occasion I'm thinking of is what we call the Last Supper, then you'll want to tell me it was more than a disappointment. It was a tragedy. Hanging over the whole event was the grim possibility that the man at the head of the table – Jesus of Nazareth – who'd spent three years of his life preaching, healing and teaching about God and

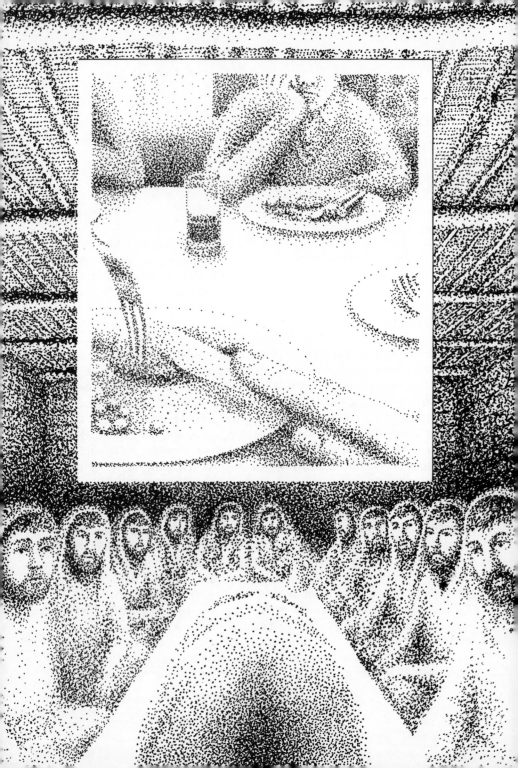

love and goodness, would find himself betrayed by one of his own men, arrested, tortured and executed.

Funnily enough, he'd seen it coming. People don't like change much. It's too disturbing. They prefer the security of old and familiar ways. The Jews of the day had their laws and traditions, and knew where they were with them. *An eye for an eye, and a tooth for a tooth.* That was justice. It saw to it that no one was punished more than he deserved. But the trouble with Jesus was he didn't see justice in quite such precise terms. He talked of love, reconciliation and forgiveness, even of your *enemies*. You couldn't talk like that in the Israel of two thousand years ago. It threatened the whole fabric of society, undermined law and order. So – the only way to be rid of this revolutionary talk was to take the man to court on some trumped-up charge, and have him put to death.

Jesus must have sensed the opposition to him growing. He had either to run for it, or make up his mind to face what was coming with no regrets or resentment, by convincing himself that something positive and good was sure to come out of it.

All the same, after supper, in the garden where he thought and prayed, and summoned up the resolve he needed to face the inevitable, he was like any one of us. He didn't want to go through with it. 'My Father,' he prayed, 'If it be possible, let this cup pass from me.' Or to put it the way you and I might have said it: 'Isn't there any way out?'

There wasn't. In the end he said, 'Not my will then, but yours be done.' It was a matter of conscience, courage and commitment, and the belief that his death was not the end, but would have the effect of releasing the power to enable the friends who'd been with him round that table to carry on the struggle where he'd left off – for love, mercy and peace to prevail in a world of mistrust and violence.

And today's Christians have inherited that struggle, and the hopes that go with it. They don't always find trouble or tragedy any easier to face than anyone else, but at least, encouraged by Jesus' example they can say, 'Come on, it's not the end of the world,' and *believe* it.

Seeing and Believing

That very day two of them were going to a village named Emmaus about seven miles from Jerusalem, and talking with each other about all these things that had happened. While they were talking and discussing together, Jesus himself drew near and went with them. But their eyes were kept from recognizing him.

When he was at table with them, he took the bread and blessed, and broke it, and gave it to them. And their eyes were opened and they recognized him and he vanished out of their sight (Luke 24.13–16, 30–31).

Standing in a queue at the baker's shop, just the right combination of smells – warm, yeasty bread, vanilla cream and icing sugar – and I find that I'm standing instead on the pavement by the open street-level shutters of a bakery from which that delicious smell had first wafted up to me when I was a boy.

It doesn't need much to bring the past flooding back in ways that are sometimes gladdening, sometimes disturbing and often a mixture of both. Sometimes, for instance, looking in a mirror when my hair needs an urgent trip to the barber's, the greyness and unkempt springiness of it remind me of the way my father's hair used to look; and suddenly I see, not my own reflection, but my father's face looking back at me.

Glimpses, smells, sounds, actions, all trivial in themselves can trigger off in anyone moments of recognition that bring what you thought was long dead and gone, back into the present, real and living. You never quite leave the past behind you. Even though its incidents

are well buried in the mind's subconscious, they have a habit of surfacing unexpectedly, raising old regrets or reviving fond memories.

Once, in a meal at the end of a long walk together, two friends sharing a loaf, suddenly saw their old friend Jesus again, the vision of him evoked by the simple act of breaking bread. They had watched him break bread and say grace when they'd eaten with him in the past. They knew he was dead now, but just for an instant, he was with them again.

It's asking for trouble, I know, to look at the story like this. People expect a Christian to say that the risen Jesus had a real flesh and blood body, that he *physically* lived again; but you only have to read the story for yourself in all its versions. There's so much coming and going through locked doors and so many vanishing tricks, and so many times when people who'd known him closely saw him again without realizing who it was, you can't help but conclude that those who wrote about it weren't primarily interested in the facts.

If you must have a miracle with a capital M, I don't think the resurrection of Jesus Christ is the place to look. I mean, if you could prove how it was done, and produce the evidence that showed how a crucified body was resuscitated and repaired, it wouldn't be a miracle any more. The real miracle is that one man's life made such an impact on the little world he lived in that it still gives inspiration and direction to people's lives, two thousand years later, worldwide.

After all, it wasn't exactly hot-off-the-press. It wasn't making headlines, as news does today, only a few hours after it happened. Thirty or forty years had passed before the gospel-writers got to work, by which time what they wrote was coloured by the tradition and mystery that had grown up. This story of the two men who invited Jesus in to share a meal with them lends wonderful support to the *mystery* of Jesus' presence recognized in the frequent ceremony of breaking bread and drinking wine which the early Christian church used to commemorate the last, sad time they'd had supper with someone they had known, admired and loved.

The facts of the matter took second place to faith, and to visions of life as it might be one day, if the impact that Jesus had made on that little Galilean community was kept so very much alive, it would reach and influence a wider world. They kept his memory alive in the worship and ritual of the Christian church, but more importantly they kept alive the truths he stood for.

Here was a man, often at odds with the bureaucracy of his day, who

98

was interested to such an extent in the *spirit* of the law that he made the *letter* of it look foolish when it refused to take circumstances or the individual into account. Here was a man who cared for the sick and the poor, and who saw the potential for good in *everyone* – you might even say *the potential for God*.

For it seems to me that the gospel stories, telling of the resurrection of Jesus, are about the potential for God that there is in every man and every woman, rich or poor, strong or weak, talented or limited – a potential that God will never allow to die. The stories tell of moments of recognition in the garden, by the seashore, in the old upper room where the disciples and Jesus often used to meet – all their familiar haunts, places which, Christians would believe, God in the shape of Jesus, deliberately came to inhabit, to be so completely a part of human life, that those with their eyes sufficiently open would see him at the heart of everything.

The Christian then, who believes in the resurrection of Jesus, is saying that he recognizes in ordinary, everyday human experience, the possibilities for good, refusing to be disheartened or defeated. The Christian believes in the potential for God that there is in himself and in other people, which means that there is no one in the whole world who can be classed as worthless, that grief and despair are not insurmountable, and death is nothing to be afraid of.

That very famous Christian St Paul, commenting on the resurrection story, went so far as to say that death had been destroyed. The Christian, whatever his mental reservations, is simply repeating the truth of that when he says *Jesus lives!*

Wind and Fire

When the day of Pentecost had come they were all together in one place. And suddenly a sound came from heaven like the rush of a mighty wind, and it filled all the house where they were sitting. And there appeared to them tongues as of fire, distributed and resting on each one of them. And they were filled with the Holy Spirit and began to speak in other tongues as the spirit gave them utterance (Acts 2.1–4).

When the open coal fire wouldn't burn, my mother would hold a newspaper over the front of the fireplace, concentrating the draught beneath the grate into a fiercer rush of air that, after a bit, made the sticks catch and crackle with flame. She'd often hold the newspaper in place until she could hear the fire roaring away behind it, and if she was ever distracted, the newspaper caught alight too and had to be hurriedly added to the blaze in the grate. Effective but risky.

I remember once the chimney itself caught fire. All we could do was stand in the street and watch with childish wonder the bright yellow flames shooting out of the chimney pot and the clouds of sooty smoke filling the sky. Before long it burned itself out, but the people who lived across the road once had to call the fire brigade to theirs. It was after dark too. For the children gathered in the street to watch the fun, it was better than Fireworks Night.

Wind and fire make an exciting, if dangerous combination, so it isn't any wonder to me that an amazing change that once took place in the lives of a group of unhappy men was described in terms of wind and fire.

The men concerned were disciples of Jesus of Nazareth. For three years they had followed him around, listened to his preaching and teaching, watched his acts of compassion and healing, and admired his readiness to do battle with the pettiness and red tape of authority. Here was a hero they would gladly follow for the rest of their days. Then tragedy struck. The authorities ganged up against him, took him to court, paid a few rogues to blacken his character with lies and executed him like a common criminal. Fifty days later, they were skulking in a house in Jerusalem feeling sorry and lost.

He'd given them a vision of what the world might be like one day if people loved instead of hated each other, if they based their lives on trust instead of suspicion. He'd been their inspiration. Now he was gone. The fire in their lives had suddenly gone out. Then they realized. If Jesus wasn't there, then it was up to them. People who suffer bereavement learn gradually to pick up their lives again and often, without discarding fond memories, begin to make the most of the lives they still have to live. If belonging to someone brings a kind of freedom as well as responsibility then, when the shock of their death is fading, a new freedom and a new responsibility begin to take their place. Life doesn't have to come to a grinding halt.

Any Christian will tell you that the way the disciples stopped feeling sorry for themselves and began to reach out to other people, is a re-enactment of the resurrection story that lies at the heart of a Christian's faith. That room, the author says – a doctor by the name of Luke – was filled with a roaring wind, and the heads of the men were lit with tongues of flame. Trying to recapture vividly the moment, he pictured them perhaps as the haloed saints of the Christian church's birth. Filled with a new and unstoppable enthusiasm they raced down the stairs into the street to share their enlightenment with anyone who cared to stop and listen, and as it happened, the city was full of foreigners enjoying the equivalent of an ancient Jewish Bank Holiday, the Feast of Pentecost.

What started then became a church which at a recent count numbered over seven hundred millions, worldwide. Not that they would have wanted the credit. They would have given that to the power of God that Christians call the Holy Spirit – the breath of God, if you like; which, when faith is dwindling and spirits are low can revive them, turning despair into hope, listlessness into energy, and a tragic

past into an ever-brightening present and a promising future.

The fire of God never dies. That *divine spark* which some poet or other reckons to be in each one of us is always capable of being fanned again into a mighty blaze.

About Turn

'As I made my journey and drew near to Damascus, about noon a great light from heaven suddenly shone about me. And I fell to the ground and heard a voice saying to me, "Saul, Saul, why do you persecute me?" And I answered, "Who are you, Lord?" And he said to me, "I am Jesus of Nazareth whom you are persecuting." Now those who were with me saw the light but did not hear the voice of the one who was speaking to me. And I said, "What shall I do, Lord?" And the Lord said to me, "Rise and go into Damascus, and there you will be told all that is appointed for you to do." And when I could not see because of the brightness of that light, I was led by the hand by those who were with me, and came into Damascus' (Acts 22.6–11).

I have this incredible sense of direction! A quick glance at the map and I can find my way almost anywhere, as long as there are one or two reassuring signposts on the way.

If you know where you are and where you're headed for it's simple enough to point your car in more or less the right direction and steer by instinct. Really? No, not really. Instinct sometimes lets you down; like the time I decided to make an interesting detour across the fens between Spalding and Kings Lynn. We came to a junction where the signpost had mysteriously disappeared. Perhaps there'd never been one.

The map that I carried in my head had Kings Lynn in the top left-hand corner of it, so naturally enough, I turned left. The trouble is that roads across the fens with all their twists and turns can turn an imaginary map upside-down and inside-out without your realizing it. Left and right no longer equate with east and west. (That's travelling south. Northbound it's the other way about.) Not that it matters. I drove merrily on, with all the confidence of someone heading in the right direction, and within a few minutes we were back at the junction we'd only just left. With only the merest hint of a chuckle in her voice, my wife said, 'I think we've been here before.' The personification of restraint she was. At least the choice of route was now self-evident.

It made me realize how glad I am that I'm not faced with the kinds of decisions that have to be made by captains of industry or cabinet ministers. Society at large is a lot less forgiving than a wife in the passenger seat of a car at a junction with no signpost. I'd hate to be a politician, recorded for posterity on video as preferring a certain course of action, and being caught out, possibly years later, heading in the opposite direction. Never mind that he'd had the sense to realize the folly of one policy and substitute another. The press a would have a field-day; but they'd be no less critical, I dare say, if he'd stuck to the original policy, justifying it and brazening it out. Who'd be in public life? For want of an Aunt Sally, people will translate firm resolve as pigheadedness, and a change of course as weakness. You can't win.

When you think about it, St Paul, that famous Christian letter-writer, being a man of some prominence – well-educated, a lawyer, Jew of good standing and free-born Roman Citizen – put all this entitlement to great respect at serious risk when he made that dramatic U-turn of his on the road to Damascus.

There he was, equipped with letters of authority from the High Priest, pursuing with great determination the Christians who'd fled to Damascus for their lives. No small factor in Saul's grim resolve was his effort to shed the haunting memory of the violent scene in which a young Christian called Stephen had been stoned to death and yet, in the very act of dying, had spoken words of forgiveness for the mob that killed him. Saul had been keeping an eye on their coats at the time. The last words and serene face of the dying Stephen must have troubled him. Clearly there was something worth dying for at the heart of this new religion. Did it deserve to be persecuted out of existence?

As he asked himself this question it was as though the voice of Jesus of Nazareth himself was doing the asking, and when the dark turmoil of Saul's inward struggle was suddenly broken by a brilliant flash of lightning that almost blinded him, he realized with great certainty that he was heading in the wrong direction. He must become a Christian.

It was no simple matter. He risked the anger of the authorities he was working for, and when, of all things, he asked to join the Christian community whose members he'd been pursuing, jailing and putting to death, they were, not surprisingly, suspicious. When, at last, they did accept him, they found him a force to be reckoned with. By sea and land, with missionary zeal, and the same energy he'd once used to put Christians down, he took Christianity beyond the borders of Israel to the far corners of the known first-century world, often using his privileged status and knowledge as a Pharisee or Roman citizen to escape a flogging or imprisonment, but frequently suffering both for his outspokenness.

What angered his critics most was his disregard for the laws and traditions which, as a Pharisee, his duty was to observe religiously. To Saul, now calling himself Paul, the Pharisees' view that God was theirs and theirs alone was sheer arrogance, a conservatism – with a small 'c' that made life drab and unadventurous, making God an equally dry old stick with nothing better to do than hand out punishments to those who upset convention.

He'd been the same once. It explained his energetic pursuit of the Christians, but now a vision that had once been inspired by too fixed an obsession with the small print of Jewish Law had been transformed into a broad vision of a God who loved even foreigners and law-breakers. A narrow path had become a highway, and this man Paul, once headed in the direction that most people approved of, risked the loss of face, condemnation and suspicion that his change of heart was certain to bring.

Most people, I'd guess, would have played it safe, choosing instead the road that would take them round in dull circles back to where they'd started from, suppressing the uncomfortable truth for the sake of a quiet life, preserving pride or status by refusing to eat humble pie.

Christians, of course, would know better than that. If Paul's example isn't enough, they've the higher example of Jesus to fix their sights on. Not that example is any guarantee. As Jesus well knew *the spirit is willing, but the flesh is weak*. The consolation for the Christian is that when he puts God, so to speak, in the passenger seat, he's with him as he goes nonchalantly down the wrong road, and still there, when he comes to his senses, to urge him along the right one.

Foreign Food for Thought

The next day, as they were on their journey and coming near the city, Peter went up on the housetop to pray, about the sixth hour. And he became hungry and desired something to eat; but while they were preparing it, he fell into a trance and saw the heaven opened, and something descending, like a great sheet, let down by four corners upon the earth. In it were all kinds of animals and reptiles and birds of the air. And there came a voice to him, 'Rise, Peter; kill and eat.' But Peter said, 'No, Lord; for I have never eaten anything that is common or unclean.' And the voice came to him a second time, 'What God has cleansed you must not call common.' This happened three times, and the thing was taken up at once to heaven (Acts 10.9–16).

The vegetarians came to dinner. We didn't mock their eccentricity of diet; they were family after all, and they'd come by invitation to help us celebrate our silver wedding. Not that we ignored their preference all together. If it could be done without embarrassment and not too much confusion in the kitchen we were ready to accommodate them.

Still, they were with us for a whole weekend, which stretches culinary ingenuity rather far, so we decided for the celebration dinner on the Saturday evening to go Chinese. The Take-Away was just a short car ride into town, and the prospect of beansprouts, bamboo shoots and noodles seemed a safe, and un-carnivorous compromise. But we ran into trouble. Quantity, that was the problem; choosing enough for four without becoming monotonous and bland.

At last, seeing the problem, one vegetarian ventured a gesture of goodwill and, setting principle aside, said, 'Look, I think our ideology is getting in the way. It doesn't matter, really.' So with great speed and relish we plumped for Special Fried Rice, heavily loaded with chunks of ham and garnished with slices of roast duck. When it arrived I tucked in, failing to notice whether the vegetarians were tempted by it or not. In any case, I respected their right to eat the food of their choice as long as I wasn't restricted by it; though I guess I respected the shedding of principle for the sake of good relations rather more.

Mind you, the vegetarianism was a recent acquisition. It must be a great deal harder to shift your position on beliefs you've grown up with. For the Jews, for instance, there were clean and unclean animals, and their religious laws forbade them to eat the meat of unclean ones. Cattle or sheep were OK, pigs and rabbits were not. The ancient Jews, knowing their books of law by heart would have been able to recite for you a whole zoo of animals, birds and shellfish that weren't allowed to find their way into the cooking pot. The reasons were probably as much to do with health and hygiene as religion, but they claimed it was what God had said. They would. Believing they were God's chosen people made them think that about most things. By the same rule, foreigners were unclean. After all, God hadn't chosen *them*. It went without saying, then, that foreigners were inferior. Gentiles they were called – non-Jews, non-persons, nobodies.

It was, then, quite a revolutionary thought that came to the mind of that famous apostle Peter, when he decided that perhaps foreigners weren't such a bad lot after all. Up on the roof of his friend Simon's house while dinner was being got ready downstairs, and feeling a little faint with hunger already, I'd guess he dozed off under the sun-blind which, as he slept and dreamed, took on the appearance of a great sheet being let down from the sky. In it he saw a whole menagerie of unclean animals, and heard a voice commanding him to kill and eat.

Do *what*? As if it wasn't enough already to be staying with Simon, a tanner by trade, whose handling of animal carcases made him, by law, unclean; here was a voice which he took to be the voice of God, telling him to eat unclean animals. Impossible. Not the done thing at all. Yet the voice insisted that God did not think of them as unclean.

The message was unmistakeable. The foreigners that Peter's upbringing and tradition had taught were not fit even to be spoken to, were to be recruited into the Christian church. You have to ask if this early sales-rep for the Christian faith hadn't simply seen the obvious way to increase his share of the religious market, or you could say that a vision is when God helps someone to see what's been staring him in the face all the time.

108

What Peter concluded was that God had no favourites. Most of us like to think he has, with us at the top of the list. It's only human nature to suppose that if there's a God, it's our ideas about living that he'll find most acceptable, if only because *we* think they're the best. We're terrific at standing on our rights, demanding what we're *entitled* to, and assuming with a fierce national pride that *British is Best*.

It would, of course, be as much a sin to do yourself down as to put yourself on a pedestal, so patriotism and pride in our achievements is fine as long as it isn't so blinkered it belittles what other people do.

The belief that worries me most is set in the climate of Cold Wars and nuclear weapons debates. We're ready to think of other people as potential enemies. We'd be mortally offended if we thought *they* looked upon *us* as potential enemies of *theirs*. It would no doubt come as a shock to see ourselves as they see us, assuming our integrity and status is superior just because we are who we are. Attitudes we've clung to for so long because we thought they were matters of principle, or because we never actually thought about them at all, become in a new age or climate of opinion the stubborn prejudices that are hindrances to good relations. 'In truth,' said Peter, coming out of his daydream and his bigotry, 'I have come to understand that God has no favourites, but that in every nation, he who fears him and acts righteously is acceptable to him.'

Visions and Voices

And I saw a beast rising out of the sea, with ten horns and seven heads, with ten diadems upon its horns and a blasphemous name upon its heads. And the beast that I saw was like a leopard, its feet were like a bear's, and its mouth was like a lion's mouth. And to it the dragon gave his power and his throne and great authority.

And the beast was given a mouth uttering haughty and blasphemous words, and it was allowed to exercise authority for forty-two months; it opened its mouth to utter blasphemies against God, blaspheming his name and his dwelling, that is, those who dwell in heaven.

Then I saw another beast which rose out of the earth; it had two horns like a lamb and it spoke like a dragon. It exercises all the authority of the first beast in its presence, and makes the earth and its inhabitants worship the first beast, whose mortal wound was healed.

Also it causes all, both small and great, both rich and poor, both free and slave, to be marked on the right hand or the forehead, so that no one can buy or sell unless he has the mark, that is, the name of the beast or the number of its name. This calls for wisdom: let him who has understanding reckon the number of the beast, for it is a human number, its number is six hundred and sixty-six (Revelation 13.1–2,5–6,11–12,16–18).

If I told you I once saw a camel, you'd believe it, wouldn't you? If I told you I'd watched it emerge from the inside of my father's army-issue kit-bag, you'd think I meant a toy camel. You'd be wrong. It was the real thing!

First came the head, pushing up the canvas flap, peering out with the half-lowered eyelids and wide nostrils of a camel's unique brand of distaste and disdain, followed by a shaggy neck, and then by the cumbersome unfolding of one gangly, knobbly-kneed leg after another, planting the front two down on the patterned linoleum, so as to rise, double-humped and dusty, full-size out of the kit-bag into the living room.

It was, of course, a dream, and I remember waking up crying. Not because I was frightened by the camel. I don't think I could even say what my emotions were. I remember the dream so vividly, I'd guess, because it was part of the uncertainty and insecurity which, being a child I could not then have put into words but which now, I suspect, had to do with my father's absence, doing his bit for King and country in Algeria during the Second World War. He'd written to say, amongst other things, that when he came home he'd have to bring something else instead of the camel he'd promised, as the camel wouldn't fit into his kit-bag. So a dream was shattered.

Funny things dreams. Like jokes. Terry Lucas told me a couple in the playground. 'Do three policemen's feet make a Scotland yard?' he wanted to know. There was no answer to that, so he pressed on, 'What do you get if you dial 666?' I didn't know. 'A policeman standing on his head.'

You get it, I trust. You have to understand that 666 is 999 upside down, and you have to know, of course, that 999 is the number to ring to get the Emergency Services. I suppose, in that case, you could equally get an inverted ambulance or fire engine. Never mind. Back to the dream, which you only understand if you first know about the letter from Algiers. Dreams and jokes alike depend for their meaning on associations – of words, of knowledge or experience, and on the split-second responses of the brain that link one idea with another. It's the kind of human electronics that the Bible's Book of Revelation depends on, though to make complete sense of it you'd have had to have lived at the time it was written – round about 96 AD.

It's a book chock-full of strange dreams and monsters. No camels as far as I remember, but plenty of dragons, serpents, horned beasts and wild horses, breathing smoke, devouring babies and heaping all manner of curses and insults upon the world and its Creator. No Loch Ness monster could hope to compete with the horrors of this lot. And they came from the lurid imagination of a man calling himself John, though it's a hundred to one that John was just a pen-name adopted to save his skin. He was in exile on the island of Patmos, imprisoned for being a Christian.

He was lucky, I suppose, to be alive, for Christians everywhere were being persecuted by the Romans. Setting out to conquer the world, Roman emperors set themselves up as gods and expected to be worshipped. Christians refused, so they were imprisoned, flogged, crucified, thrown to the lions, and suffered a multitude of other ingenious forms of torture.

When John – we'll have to go on calling him that – wrote his Book of Revelation, it was to give some encouragement to the hard-pressed Christians in the seven churches throughout Asia, and his visions were a kind of code that the Christians would have understood at once, but which would leave the Romans mystified, protecting the author from possible retribution.

Funnily enough, 666 was part of the code. It stood for the emperor Nero – you know the one; he was renowned for practising his fiddle while the city was going up in flames. Of all Roman emperors, his reign of terror was more cruel than any other. In John's day a different but equally ruthless emperor was ruling, and it seemed to John as though Nero had returned. These two scourges of the first century AD were the two beasts he wrote about, the persecutors or Antichrists who desecrated everything and everyone in their lust for total power.

Religious cranks in our own time who let their imaginations run even more amok than John and think, so to speak, that dialling 666 will call up the devil have the makings of a good horror movie but you can't take it any more seriously than that. More to the point is that John seemed to know, either from experience or divine insight that great empires built by force and maintained by oppression were destined eventually to crumble. All the Christians had to do was wait.

Mind you, they had to wait another three centuries before the Roman Empire finally collapsed, and patience and endurance are poor consolation when your choice of religion puts your life at risk. Couldn't he offer something better than *that*? Well, sort of. He envisaged a day when God would establish a new heaven and a new earth, when pain and tears would be no more, when there would be a peace like no peace ever known before, that needed no powerful ruler to control it, only the power of God which Christians know is something different altogether.

On the one hand, there's the kind of power that feeds the greed and ambition of men and women whose lack of confidence and character

needs the ego-boosting sensation of controlling other people's lives. They need to be waited upon and looked up to, an obsession that reveals their inner emptiness and desperation. But there's another kind of power. Christians would say you could see it most clearly in the life of Jesus of Nazareth, a man unconcerned with status or possessions, but deeply concerned for people as individuals. Christians, thinking of him as both God and human being, see him effectively turning the idea of power upside down. Instead of expecting to be waited upon, he thought of himself as a servant. Instead of expecting to be looked up to, he made those he met feel that *they* were worth something. And he believed that this power – the power of *love* – was the only power worth dying for, not least because it seemed to him to be a way of releasing that power into the lives of other people. It's what Christians mean when they think of Jesus as living again. What they call *resurrection* is the power of love constantly being re-energized, used up, and re-energized again. Over and over.

So the Christian believes that the destiny of humankind is firmly in the hands of God who chooses to release his unique sort of power through the ordinary men and women in his world who use it in the humble service of their workmates, friends and neighbours and, if pressed, to console the heartache or relieve the pain of those they might be tempted to think of as their enemies too.

It's not the kind of power that produces an explosion of instant results. When John offered a kind of Utopia to the readers of the Book of Revelation, he couldn't say how soon or late it would come. So Christians go on waiting, but faithfully believing that the power never flags, for John also had a vision of a God who was the beginning and end of all things.

Love is the slow, patient, painstaking, suffering, resilient, enduring power that, given time, can defeat the *Beasts* of this or any other century, who think they can control the destinies of people by human law or force of arms.

No one has ever put it better than St. Paul:

Love is patient and kind; love is not jealous or boastful; it is not arrogant or rude. Love does not insist on its own way; it is not irritable or resentful; it does not rejoice at wrong, but rejoices in the right. Love bears all things, believes all things, hopes all things, endures all things. Lover never ends (I Corinthians 13.4–8a).